Allyn & Bacon Casebook Series
Adoption

Edited by

Jerry L. Johnson
Grand Valley State University

George Grant, Jr.
Grand Valley State University

Boston New York San Francisco
Mexico City Montreal Toronto London Madrid Munich Paris
Hong Kong Singapore Tokyo Cape Town Sydney

To all of those who have helped, advised, supported, criticized,
and forgiven. You know who you are.
Jerry L. Johnson

To my wife, Beverly, who inspires and supports me
in all my endeavors. In loving memory of my father and mother,
George and Dorothy Grant, and Daisy Franks.
George Grant, Jr.

Series Editor: *Patricia Quinlin*
Marketing Manager: *Kris Ellis-Levy*
Production Administrator: *Janet Domingo*
Compositor: *Galley Graphics*
Composition Buyer: *Linda Cox*
Manufacturing Buyer: *JoAnne Sweeney*
Cover Coordinator: *Rebecca Krzyzaniak*

For related titles and support materials, visit our online catalog at www.ablongman.com.

Library of Congress Cataloging-in-Publication Data

Allyn & Bacon casebook series for adoption / edited by Jerry L. Johnson & George Grant, Jr.—1st ed.
p. cm.
Includes bibliographical references.
ISBN 0-205-38954-6 (pbk.)
1. Adoption—Case studies. 2. Child welfare—Case studies. 3. Family social work—Case studies. 4. Social case work. I. Title: Allyn and Bacon casebook series for adoption. II. Title: Casebook series for adoption. III. Johnson, Jerry L. IV. Grant, George, Jr.
HV875. A43 2005
362.734—dc22

2004053488

Printed in the United States of America

10 9 8 7 6 5 4 3 2 1 09 08 07 06 05 04

Contents

Preface

This text offers students the chance to study the work of experienced social workers practicing with children and families in various phases of the adoption process. As graduate and undergraduate social work educators, we (the editors) have struggled to find quality practice materials that translate well into a classroom setting. Over the years, we have used case materials from our practice careers, professionally produced audio-visuals, and tried other casebooks. While each had its advantages, we could not find a vehicle that allowed students to study the work of experienced practitioners that took students beyond the belief that practice is a technical endeavor that involves finding "correct" interventions to solve client problems.

We want our students to study and analyze how experienced practitioners think about practice and how they struggle to resolve ethical dilemmas and make treatment decisions that meet the needs of their clientele. We want students to review and challenge the work of others in a way that allows them to understand what comprises important practice decisions with real clients in real practice settings. That is, we want classroom materials that allow students entry into the minds of experienced practitioners.

Goals of the Casebook

This Casebook focuses on practice with clients dealing with adoption in a variety of settings and from diverse backgrounds. Our goal is to provide students with an experience that:

1. Provides personal and intimate glimpses into the thinking and actions of experienced practitioners as they work with clients. In each case, students may demonstrate their understanding of the cases and how and/or why the authors approached their case in the manner presented.

2. Provides a vehicle to evaluate the process, ideas, and methods used by the authors. We also wanted to provide students a chance to present their ideas about how they would have worked differently with the same case.
3. Affords students the opportunity to use evidence-based practice findings (Gibbs, 2003; Cournoyer, 2004) as part of the case review and planning process. We challenge students to base practice judgments and case planning exercises on current practice evidence available through library and/or electronic searches, and practice wisdom gained through consultation and personal experience when the evidence is conflicted or lacking.

To meet our goals, the cases we included in this text focus on the practice *process,* specifically client engagement, assessment, and the resultant clinical process, including the inevitable ethical dilemmas that consistently arise in daily practice. We aim to demonstrate the technical and artistic elements involved in developing and managing the various simultaneous processes involved in practice. While we recognize the difficulty of presenting process information (circular) in a linear medium (book), we have tried to do the best job possible toward this end.

To achieve our goals, we include four in-depth case studies in this text. In these case studies, authors guide students through the complete practice process, from initial contact to client termination and practice evaluation. Focusing heavily on multi-systemic client life history (see Chapter 1), students get a detailed look into the life history and presentation of the client. Then, we challenge students to "finish the case" by using client information and classroom learning to develop a written narrative assessment, diagnostic statement, treatment and intervention plan, termination and follow-up plan, and a plan to evaluate practice. We have used these cases as in-class exercises, the basis for semester-long term papers, and as comprehensive final examinations that integrate multifaceted student learning in practice courses across the curriculum.

Rationale

As former practitioners, we chose the cases carefully. Therefore, the cases in this text focus on the process (thinking, planning, and decision-making) of social work practice and not necessarily on techniques or outcome. Do not be fooled by this statement. Obviously, we believe in successful client outcome based, at least in part, on the use of evidence-based practice methods and current research findings. As important as this is, it is not our focus here—with good reason. Our experience suggests that instructive process occurs in cases that have successful and unsuccessful outcome. In fact, we often learned more from unsuccessful cases than successful cases. We learned the most when events did not play out as planned. While some of the cases terminated successfully, others did not. This is not a commentary on the author or the author's skill level. Everyone has cases (sometimes too many) that do not turn out as planned. We chose cases based on one simple criterion: did it provide the best possible hope for practice education? We asked authors to teach practice by considering cases that were interesting and difficult, regardless of outcome. We did not want the Casebook to become simply a vehicle to promote practice brilliance.

Mostly, we wanted this text to differ from other casebooks, because we were unsatisfied with casebooks as teaching tools. As part of the process of planning our Casebooks, we reviewed other casebooks and discussed with our graduate and undergraduate students approaches that best facilitated learning in the classroom. We discovered that many students were also dissatisfied with a casebook approach to education, for a variety of reasons. Below, we briefly address what our students told us about casebooks in general.

1. *Linear presentation.* One of the most significant problems involves case presentation. Generally, this involves two issues: linearity and brevity. Most written case studies give students the impression that practice actually proceeds smoothly, orderly, and in a sequential manner. These cases often leave students believing—or expecting—that clinical decisions are made beforehand and that practice normally proceeds as planned. In other words, students often enter the field believing that casework follows an "*A, leads to B, leads to C, leads to clients living happily ever after*" approach.

Experienced practitioners know better. In over 40 years of combined social work practice in a variety of settings, we have learned—often the "hard way"—that the opposite is true. We rarely, if ever, had a case proceed sequentially, whether our client is an individual, couple, family, group, community, or classroom. That is, the process of engagement (including cultural competence), assessment, treatment planning, intervention, and follow-up occur in a circular manner, rooted in the client's social, physical, and cultural context, and includes consideration of the practitioner, his or her organization, and the laws and policies that affect and/or determine the boundaries of social work practice and treatment funding.

Practice evolves in discontinuous cycles over time, including time-limited treatments mandated by the managed care system. Therefore, real-life clinical practice—just as in all developing human relationships—seems to consistently require stops and starts, take wrong turns, and even, in some cases, require "do-overs." While the goal of competent practice is to facilitate an orderly helping process that includes planned change (Timberlake, Farber, & Sabatino, 2002), practice, as an orderly process, is more often a goal (or a myth) than planned certainty. Given the linearity of case presentations discussed above, readers are often left without an appreciation or understanding of practice as process.

Additionally, many of the case presentation texts we reviewed provided "hard" client data and asked students to develop treatment plans based on this data. Yet, as any experienced practitioner knows, the difficulty in practice occurs during engagement and data collection. The usual case approach often overlooks this important element of practice. While a book format limits process writing, we believe that the case format we devised here brings students closer to the "real thing."

2. *Little focus on client engagement.* As we like to remind students, there are two words in the title of our profession: social and work. In order for the "work" to be successful, students must learn to master the "social"—primarily client engagement and relationship building. Social work practice is relationship based (Saleebey, 2002) and, from our perspective, relies more on the processes involved in relationship building and client engagement than technical intervention skills (Johnson, 2004). Successful practice is often rooted more in the ability of practitioners to develop open and trusting relationships with client(s) than on their ability to employ specific methods of intervention (Johnson, 2004).

Yet, this critically important element of practice often goes understated or ignored. Some texts even assume that engagement skills somehow exist before learning about practice. We find this true in casebooks and primary practice texts as well. When it is discussed, engagement and relationship building is presented as a technical process that also proceeds in linear fashion. Our experience with students, employees, and practitioner/trainees over the last two decades suggests that it is wrong to assume that students and/or practitioners have competent engagement or relationship building skills. From our perspective, developing a professional relationship that involves trust and openness, where clients feel safe to dialogue about the most intimate and sometimes embarrassing events in their lives, is the primary responsibility of the practitioner, and often spells the difference between positive and negative client outcome (Johnson, 2004; Miller & Rollnick, 2002; Harper & Lantz, 1996). Hence, each case presentation tries to provide a sense of this difficult and often elusive process and some of the ways that the authors overcame challenges to the culturally competent client engagement process.

Target Audience

Our target audience for this text, and the others in the series, are advanced undergraduate as well as foundation and advanced graduate students in social work and other helping disciplines. We have tested our approach with students at several different points in their education. We find that the casebooks can be used as:

- An adjunct learning tool for undergraduates preparing for or already involved in their field practicum.
- Practice education and training for foundation-level graduate students in practice theory and/or methods courses.
- An adjunct learning tool for second-year graduate students in field practicum.
- An adjunct learning tool for undergraduate and/or graduate students in any practice courses pertaining to specific populations.

While we are social work educators, we believe the casebooks will be useful in social work and other disciplines in the human services, including counseling psychology, counseling, mental health, psychology, and specialty disciplines such as marriage and family therapy, substance abuse, and mental health degree or certificate programs. Any educational or training program designed to prepare students to work with clients in a helping capacity may find the casebooks useful as a learning tool.

Structure of Cases

We organized the case studies to maximize critical thinking, the use of professional literature, evidenced-based practice knowledge, and classroom discussion in the learning process. At various points throughout each case, we comment on issues and/or dilemmas highlighted by the case. Our comments always end with a series of questions designed to focus student learning by calling on their ability to find and evaluate evidence from the professional literature and through classroom discussion. We ask students to collect evidence on different sides of an issue, evaluate that evidence, and develop a professional position that they can defend in writing and/or discussion with other students in the classroom or seminar setting.

We hope that you find the cases and our format as instructive and helpful in your courses as we have in ours. We have field-tested our format in courses at our university, finding that students respond well to the length, depth, and rigor of the case presentations. Universally, students report that the case materials were an important part of their overall learning process.

Organization of the Text

We organized this text to maximize its utility in any course. Chapter 1 provides an overview of the Advanced Multi-Systemic (AMS) practice approach. We provide this as one potential organizing tool for students to use while reading and evaluating the subsequent cases. This chapter offers students an organized and systematic framework to use when analyzing cases and/or formulating narrative assessments, treatment, and intervention plans. Our intent is to provide a helpful tool, not make a political statement about the efficacy or popularity of one practice framework versus others. In fact, we invite faculty and students to apply whatever practice framework they wish when working the cases.

In Chapter 2, *George Grant, Jr., Ph.D., MSW* presents his work in **Sarah and Robert.** Sarah and Robert were siblings, thrust into the foster care and adoptive systems after their parents died in a murder-suicide. Their experiences in multiple placements, caused by their emotional and behavioral reactions to the violence in their lives, provide readers with insight into the difficulties in special needs adoption. Grant, Jr., provides in-depth information about the children and adoption, leaving readers to make important decisions about adoptive placement based on the case. This interactive case will challenge readers at every turn.

In Chapter 3, *Mildred Drollinger, MSW* and *Jill C. Tyler-Skinner, BA* present an interesting case about a potential disrupted adoption when the adoptive child develops behavioral problems as an adolescent. In a case entitled **The Morgan**

Family, Drollinger and Tyler-Skinner show the important role of a Post Adoption Support agency in helping adoptive families remain together as problems develop.

In Chapter 4, *Steve De Groot, Ph.D.* presents a case entitled **The Boyds.** In this case, De Groot presents a case involving a family in legal trouble for abusing their newly adopted daughters from Russia. De Groot also clearly demonstrates the complexities of the legal system and international adoption. The authors also navigate the complexities of the multi-systemic environment of professionals in child welfare that often send mixed messages.

The final chapter, **Travis,** presents the work of *Robin L. Smith, MSW* with a troubled African American male child caught in the child welfare system. Smith demonstrates the various multi-systemic issues involved with this case and guides readers through an in-depth discussion of treatment from a multi-cultural perspective. This case is also interactive. Smith presents readers a wealth of information about the case. Readers are then asked to complete a multi-systemic assessment, treatment plan, and an intervention plan.

Acknowledgments

We would like to thank the contributors to this text, Mildred Drollinger, Jill C. Tyler-Skinner, Steve De Groot, and Robin L. Smith for their willingness to allow their work to be challenged and discussed in a public venue. We would also like to thank Patricia Quinlin and her people at Allyn and Bacon for their faith in the Casebook Series and in our ability to manage fourteen manuscripts at once. Additionally, we have to thank all of our students and student assistants that served as "guinea pigs" for our case studies. Their willingness to provide honest feedback contributes mightily to this series.

Jerry L. Johnson—I want to thank my wife, Cheryl, for her support and willingness to give me the time and encouragement to write and edit. I also owe a debt of gratitude to my dear friend Hope, for being there when I need you the most.

George Grant, Jr.— I want to thank Dean Rodney Mulder, Dr. Elaine Schott, Dr. Doris Perry, and Professor Emily Jean McFadden for their insight, encouragement, and support during this process. To Lisa Neimeyer and Kimberly S. Crawford for their eye to detail. Finally, I want to thank Alice D. Denton and Alyson D. Grant for their continued support and Dr. Julius Franks and Professor Daniel Groce for their intellectual discourse and unwavering support.

Contributors

The Editors

Jerry L. Johnson, Ph.D., MSW is an Associate Professor in the School of Social Work at Grand Valley State University in Grand Rapids, Michigan. He received his

MSW from Grand Valley State University and his Ph.D. in sociology from Western Michigan University. Johnson has been in social work for more than 20 years as a practitioner, supervisor, administrator, consultant, teacher, and trainer. He was the recipient of two Fulbright Scholarship awards to Albania in 1998–99 and 2000–01. In addition to teaching and writing, Johnson serves in various consulting capacities in countries such as Albania and Armenia. He is the author of two previous books, *Crossing Borders—Confronting History: Intercultural Adjustment in a Post-Cold War World* (2000, Rowan and Littlefield) and *Fundamentals of Substance Abuse Practice* (2004, Wadsworth Brooks/Cole).

George Grant, Jr., Ph.D., MSW is an Associate Professor in the School of Social Work at Grand Valley State University in Grand Rapids, Michigan. Grant, Jr., also serves as the Director of Grand Valley State University's MSW Program. He received his MSW from Grand Valley State University and Ph.D. in sociology from Western Michigan University. Grant, Jr., has a long and distinguished career as practitioner, administrator, consultant, teacher, and trainer in social work, primarily in fields dedicated to Child Welfare.

Contributors

Robin L. Smith, MSW, ACSW is an Assistant Professor in the School of Social Work at Grand Valley State University in Grand Rapids, Michigan. She received her MSW degree from Grand Valley State University and is currently completing her Ph.D. in Social Work from Loyola University. Smith has over 13 years of practice experience, specializing in work with children and families, children and adolescent mental health with emphasis on African American male adolescents, and social work practice in schools.

Mildred Drollinger, MSW has over 25 years of experience working in the area of special needs adoption. From pre-adoption planning, adoptive placements, to post-adoption services, Drollinger has provided therapy, run support groups and workshops, and provided training to professionals in the field of adoption. She has served as a consultant to agencies and organizations dedicated to supporting special needs adoption. Drollinger received her BS and MSW from Grand Valley State University.

Jill C. Tyler-Skinner, BA has worked in child welfare, family services, and education for over 23 years. Tyler-Skinner specialized in foster care, adoption, and delinquency services. She has developed workshops and training materials, ran support groups for adoptive children and parents and consulted nationally on special needs adoption issues. Tyler-Skinner was also the Associate Director of a large children welfare agency. She had a BA and Secondary Teaching Degree from Alma College and a special education certification for Central Michigan University.

Steve De Groot, Ph.D. is a psychologist. He has been involved in the assessment and evaluation as well as treatment of numerous individuals and couples who have had their children involved in the child welfare system. For over 17 years, De Groot has been involved in working with individuals and families, and is frequently referred cases from judges and attorneys for either evaluative or therapeutic involvement. In addition, he fulfills a contract with a large social service agency, and is in private practice.

Bibliography

Cournoyer, B. R. (2004). *The evidence-based social work skills book.* Boston: Allyn and Bacon.

Gibbs, L. E. (2003). *Evidence-based practice for the helping professions: A practical guide with integrated multimedia.* Pacific Grove, CA: Brooks/Cole.

Harper, K. V., & Lantz, J. (1996). *Cross-cultural practice: Social work practice with diverse populations.* Chicago: Lyceum Books.

Johnson, J. L. (2004). *Fundamentals of substance abuse practice.* Pacific Grove, CA: Brooks/Cole.

Miller, W. R., & Rollnick, S. (2002). *Motivational interviewing: Preparing people to change addictive behavior* (2nd ed.). New York: Guilford Press.

Saleebey, D. (2002). *The strengths perspective in social work practice* (3rd ed.). Boston: Allyn and Bacon.

Timberlake, E. M., Farber, M. Z., & Sabatino, C. A. (2002). *The general method of social work practice: McMahon's generalist perspective* (4th ed.). Boston: Allyn and Bacon.

1

A Multi-Systemic Approach to Practice

Jerry L. Johnson & George Grant, Jr.

This is a practice-oriented text, designed to build practice skills with individuals, families, and groups. We intend to provide you the opportunity to study the process involved in treating real cases from the caseloads of experienced practitioners. Unlike other casebooks, we include fewer cases, but provide substantially more detail in hopes of providing a realistic look into the thinking, planning, and approach of the practitioners/authors. We challenge you to study the authors' thinking and methods to understand their approach and then use critical thinking skills and the knowledge you have gained in your education and practice to propose alternative ways of treating the same clients. In other words, what would your course of action be if you were the primary practitioner responsible for these cases? Our hope is that this text provides a worthwhile and rigorous experience studying real cases as they progressed in practice.

Before proceeding to the cases, we include this chapter as an introduction to the Advanced Multi-Systemic (AMS) practice perspective. We decided to present this introduction with two primary goals in mind. First, we want you to use the information contained in this chapter to help assess and analyze the cases in this text. You will have the opportunity to complete a multi-systemic assessment, diagnoses, treatment, and intervention plan for each case. This chapter will provide the theoretical and practical basis for this exercise. Second, we hope you find that AMS makes conceptualizing cases clearer in your practice environment. We do not suggest that AMS is the only way, or even the best way, for every practitioner to conceptualize cases. We simply know, through experience, that AMS is an effective way to think about practice with client-systems of all sizes and configurations. While there are many approaches to practice, AMS offers an effective way to place clinical decisions in the context of client lives and experiences, making engagement and treatment productive for clients and practitioners.

Advanced Multi-Systemic (AMS) Practice

Sociological Roots

> Whether the point of interest is a great power state or a minor literary mood, a family, a prison, and a creed—these are the kinds of questions the best social analysts have asked. They are the intellectual pivots of classic studies of (person) in society—and they are the questions inevitably raised by any mind possessing the sociological imagination. For that imagination is the capacity to shift from one perspective to another—from the political to the psychological; from examination of a single family to comparative assessment of the national budgets of the world; from the theological school to the military establishment; from considerations of an oil industry to studies of contemporary poetry. It is the capacity to range from the most impersonal and remote transformations to the most intimate features of the human self—and see the relations between the two. Back of its use is always the urge to know the social and historical meaning of the individual in the society and in the period in which he (or she) has his quality and his (or her) being. (Mills, 1959, p. 7; parentheses added)

Above, sociologist C. Wright Mills provided a seminal description of the sociological imagination. As it turns out, Mills's sociological imagination is also an apt description of AMS. Mills believed that linking people's "private troubles" to "public issues" (p. 2) by placing them in historical context was the most effective way to understand people and their issues. It forces investigators to contextualize individuals and families in the framework of the larger social, political, economic, and historical environments in which they live. Ironically, this is also the goal of social work practice (Germain & Gitterman, 1996; Longres, 2000). Going further, Mills (1959) stated:

> We have come to know that every individual lives, from one generation to the next, in some society; that he (or she) lives out a biography, and that he (or she) lives it out within some historical sequence. By the fact of his (or her) living he (or she) contributes, however minutely, to the shaping of this society and to the course of its history, even as he (or she) is made by society and by its historical push and shove. (p. 6)

Again, Mills was not speaking as a social worker. He was an influential sociologist, speaking about a method of social research. In *The Sociological Imagination,* Mills (1959) proposed this as a method to understand the links between people, their daily lives, and their multi-systemic environment. Yet, while laying the theoretical groundwork for social research, Mills also provided the theoretical foundation for an effective approach to social work practice. We find four relevant points in *The Sociological Imagination* that translate directly to social work practice.

1. It is crucial to recognize the relationships between people's personal issues and strengths (private troubles) and the issues (political, economic, social, historical, and legal) and strengths of the multi-systemic environment (public issues) in which people live daily and across their life span. A multi-systemic understanding includes recognizing and integrating issues and strengths at the micro (individual, family, extended kin, etc.), mezzo (local community), and macro (state, region, national, and international policy, laws, political, economic, and social) levels during client engagement, assessment, treatment, follow-up, and evaluation of practice.

2. This depth of understanding (by social workers and, especially, clients) can lead to change in people's lives. We speak here about second-order change, or, significant change that makes a long-term difference in people's lives; change that helps people view themselves differently in relationship to their world. This level of change becomes possible when people make multi-systemic links in a way that makes sense to them (Freire, 1993). In other words, clients become "empowered" to change when they understand their life in the context of their world and realize that they have previously unforeseen or unimagined choices in how they live, think, believe, and act.

3. Any assessment and/or clinical diagnoses that exclude multi-systemic links do not provide a holistic picture of people's lives, their troubles, and/or their strengths. In sociology this leads to a reductionist view of people and society, while in social work it reduces the likelihood that services will be provided (or received by clients) in a way that addresses client problems and utilizes client strengths meaningfully. The opportunity for change is reduced whenever client life history is overlooked because it does not fit, or is not called for, in a practitioner's preferred method of helping, or because of shortcuts many people believe are needed in a managed care environment. One cannot learn too much about their clients' lives, attitudes, beliefs, and values as they relate to the private troubles presented in treatment.

4. Inherent in AMS and foundational to achieving all that was discussed above relies on practitioners being able to rapidly develop rapport with clients that leads to engagement in treatment. In this text, client engagement

> . . . occurs when you develop, in collaboration with clients, a trusting and open professional relationship that promotes hope and presents viable prospects for change. Successful engagement occurs when you create a social context in which vulnerable people (who often hold jaded attitudes toward helping professionals) can share their innermost feelings, as well as their most embarrassing and shameful behavior with you, a *total stranger.* (Johnson, 2004, p. 93; emphasis in original)

AMS Overview

First, we should define two important terms that comprise AMS. Understanding these terms is important, because they provide the foundation for understanding the language and concepts used throughout the remainder of this chapter.

1. Advanced. According to Derezotes (2000), "the most advanced theory is also the most inclusive" (p. viii). AMS is advanced because it is inclusive. It requires responsible practitioners, in positions of responsibility (perhaps as solo practitioners), to acquire a depth of knowledge, skills, and self-awareness that allows for an inclusive application of knowledge acquired in the areas of human behavior in the social environment, social welfare policy, social research and practice evaluation, and multiple practice methods and approaches in service of clients and client systems of various sizes, types, and configurations.

AMS practitioners are expected to have the most inclusive preparation possible, "both the broad generalist base of knowledge, skills, and values and an in-depth proficiency in practice with selected social work methods and populations" (Derezotes, 2000, p. xii). Hence, advanced practitioners are well trained, and with in-depth knowledge, are often in positions of being responsible for clients as primary practitioners. They are afforded the responsibility for engaging, assessing, intervening, and evaluating practice, therefore ensuring that clients are ethically treated in a way that is culturally competent and respectful of their client's worldview. In other words, AMS practitioners develop the knowledge, skills, and values needed to be leaders in their organizations, communities, the social work profession, and especially in the treatment of their clients. The remainder of this chapter explains why AMS is an advanced approach to practice.

2. Multi-systemic. From the earliest moments in their education, social workers learn a systems perspective that emphasizes the connectedness between people and their problems to the complex interrelationships that exist in their client's world (Timberlake, Farber, & Sabatino, 2002). To explain these connections, systems theory emphasizes three important concepts: wholeness, relationships, and homeostasis. Wholeness refers to the notion that the various parts or elements (subsystem) of a system interact to form a whole that best describes the system in question. This concept asserts that no system can be understood or explained unless the connectedness of the subsystems to the whole are understood or explained. In other words, the whole is greater than the sum of its parts. Moreover, systems theory also posits that change in one subsystem will affect change in the system as a whole.

In terms of systems theory, relationship refers to the patterns of interaction and overall structures that exist within and between subsystems. The nature of these relationships is more important than the system itself. When trying to understand or explain a system (individual, family, organization, etc.) we should examine how subsystems connect through relationships, the characteristics of the relationships between subsystems, and how the subsystems interact provide clues to understanding the system as a whole. Hence, the application of systems theory is primarily based on understanding relationships. As someone once said about systems theory, in systems problems occur between people and subsystems (relationships), not "in" them. People's internal problems relate to the nature of the relationships in the systems where they live and interact.

Homeostasis refers to the notion that most living systems work to maintain and preserve the existing system, or the status quo. For example, family members often assume roles that serve to protect and maintain family stability, often at the expense of "needed" change. The same can be said for organizations or groups. The natural tendency toward homeostasis in systems represents what we call the "dilemma of change" (Johnson, 2004). This can best be described as the apparent conflict, or what appears to be client resistance or lack of motivation, that often occurs when clients approach moments of significant change. Systems of all types and configurations struggle with the dilemma of change: should they change to the unknown or remain the same, even if the status quo is unhealthy or unproductive? Put differently, systems strive for stability, even at the expense of health and well-being of individual members and/or the system itself.

What do we mean, then, by the term *multi-systemic*? Clients (individuals, families, etc.) are systems that interact with a number of different systems simultaneously. These systems exist and interact at multiple levels, ranging from the micro level (individual and families), the mezzo level (local community, institutions, organizations, the practitioner and their agency, etc.), to the macro level (culture, laws and policy, politics, oppression and discrimination, international events, etc.). How these various systems come together, interact, and adapt, along with the relationships that exist within and between each system work together to comprise the "whole" that is the client, or client-system. In practice, the client (individual, couple, family, etc.) is not the "system," but one of many interacting subsystems in a maze of other subsystems constantly interacting to create the system—the client plus elements from multiple subsystems at each level. It would be a mistake to view the client as the whole system. They are but one facet of a multidimensional and multi-level system comprised of the client and various other subsystems at the micro, mezzo, and macro levels.

Therefore, the term *multi-systemic* refers to the nature of a system comprised of the various multi-level subsystems described above. A multi-systemic perspective recognizes that clients are *one part or subsystem* in relationship with other subsystemic influences occurring on different levels. This level of understanding—the system as the whole produced through multi-systemic subsystem interactions—is the main unit of investigation for practice. As stated above, it is narrow to consider the client as a functioning independent system with peripheral involvement with other systems existing outside of their intimate world. These issues and relationships work together to help shape and mold the client who, in turn, shapes and molds his or her relationship to the other subsystems. Yet, the person-of-the-client is but one part of the system in question during practice.

AMS provides an organized framework for gathering, conceptualizing, and analyzing multi-systemic client data and for proceeding with the helping process. It defines the difference between social work and other disciplines in the helping professions at the level of theory and practice. How, you ask? Unlike other professional disciplines that tend to focus on one or a few domains (i.e., psychology, medicine, etc.), AMS provides a comprehensive and holistic "picture" of clients or client-systems in the context of their environment by considering information about multiple personal and systemic domains simultaneously.

Resting on the generalist foundation taught in all Council on Social Work Education (CSWE) accredited undergraduate and foundation-level graduate programs, AMS requires practitioners to contextualize client issues in the context of the multiple interactions that occur between the client/client-system and the social, economic, legal, political, and physical environment in which the client lives. It is a unifying perspective based in the client's life, history, and culture that guides the process of collecting and analyzing client life information and intervening to promote personal choice through a comprehensive, multi-systemic framework. Beginning with culturally competent client engagement, a comprehensive multi-systemic assessment points toward a holistically based treatment plan that requires practitioners to select and utilize appropriate practice theories, models, and methods—or combinations thereof—that best fit the client's unique circumstances and needs.

AMS is not a practice theory, model, or method itself. It is a perspective or framework for conceptualizing client-systems. It relies on the practitioner's ability to use a variety of theories, models, and methods, and to incorporate knowledge from human behavior, social policy, research/evaluation, and practice into his or her routine approach with clients. For example, an AMS practitioner will have the skills to apply different approaches to individual treatment (client-centered, cognitive-behavioral, etc.), family treatment (structural, narrative, Bowenian, etc.), work with couples, in groups, arrange for specialized care if needed, and as an advocate on behalf of their client. It may also require practitioners to treat clients in a multi-modal approach (i.e., individual and group treatments simultaneously).

Practitioners not only must know how to apply different approaches but also how to determine, primarily through the early engagement and assessment process, which theory, model, or approach (direct or indirect, for example) would work best for a particular client. Hence, successful practice using AMS relies heavily on the practitioner's ability to competently engage and multi-systemically assess client problems and strengths. Practitioners must simultaneously develop a sense of their client's personal interaction and relationship style—especially related to how they relate to authority figures—when determining which approach would best suit the client. For example, a reserved, quiet, or thoughtful client or someone who lacks assertiveness may not be well-served by a directive, confrontational approach, regardless of the practitioner's preference. Moreover, AMS practitioners rely on professional practice research and outcome studies to help determine which approach or intervention package might work best for particular clients and/or client-systems. AMS expects practitioners to know how to find and evaluate practice research in their practice areas or specialties.

Elements of the Advanced Multi-Systemic Approach to Social Work Practice

The advanced multi-systemic approach entails the following seven distinct, yet integrated elements of theory and practice. Each is explained below.

Ecological Systems Perspective

One important subcategory of systems therapy for social work is the ecological systems perspective. This perspective combines important concepts from the science of ecology and general systems theory into a way of viewing client problems and strengths in social work practice. In recent years, it has become the prevailing perspective for social work practice (Miley, O'Melia, & DuBois, 2004). The ecological systems perspective—sometimes referred to as the ecosystems perspective—is a useful metaphor for guiding social workers as they think about cases (Germain & Gitterman, 1980).

Ecology focuses on how subsystems work together and adapt. In ecology, adaptation is "a dynamic process between people and their environments as people grow, achieve competence, and make contributions to others" (Greif, 1986, p. 225). Insight from ecology leads to an analysis of how people fit within their environment and what adaptations are made in the fit between people and their environments. Problems develop as a function of inadequate or improper adaptation or fit between people and their environments.

General systems theory focuses on how human systems interact. It focuses specifically on how people grow, survive, change, and achieve stability or instability in the complex world of multiple systemic interactions (Miley, O'Melia, & DuBois, 2004). General systems theory has contributed significantly to the growth of the family therapy field and to how social workers understand their clients.

Together, ecology and general systems theory evolved into what social workers know as the ecological systems perspective. The ecological systems perspective provides a systemic framework for understanding the many ways that persons and environments interact. Accordingly, individuals and their individual circumstances can be understood in the context of these interactions. The ecological systems perspective provides an important part of the foundation for AMS. Miley, O'Melia, and DuBois (2004) provide an excellent summary of the ecological systems perspective. They suggest that it

1. Presents a dynamic view of human beings as system interactions in context.
2. Emphasizes the significance of human system interactions.
3. Traces how human behavior and interaction develop over time in response to internal and external forces.
4. Describes current behavior as an adaptive fit of "persons in situations."
5. Conceptualizes all interaction as adaptive or logical in context.

6. Reveals multiple options for change within persons, their social groups, and in their social and physical environments (p. 33).

Social Constructionism

To maintain AMS as an inclusive practice approach, we need to build on the ecological systems perspective by including ideas derived from social constructionism. Social constructionism builds on the ecological systems perspective by introducing ideas about how people define themselves and their environment. Social constructionism also, by definition, introduces the role of culture in the meaning people give to themselves and other systems in their multi-systemic environments. The ecological systems perspective discusses relationships at the systemic level. Social constructionism introduces meaning and value into the equation, allowing for a deeper understanding and appreciation of the nature of multi-systemic relationships and adaptations.

Usually, people assume that reality is something "out there" that hits them in the face, something that independently exists, and people must learn to "deal with it." Social constructionism posits something different. Evolving as a critique of the "one reality" belief system, social constructionism points out that the world is comprised of multiple realities. People define their own reality and then live within those definitions. Accordingly, the definition of reality will be different for everyone. Hence, social constructionism deals primarily with meaning, or the systemic processes by which people come to define themselves in their social world. As sociologist W. I. Thomas said, in what has become known as the Thomas Theorem, "If people define situations as real, they are real in their consequences."

For example, some people believe that they can influence the way computerized slot machines pay out winnings by the way they sit, the feeling they get from the machine as they look at it in the casino, by the clothes they are wearing, or by how they trigger the machine, either by pushing the button or pulling the handle. Likewise, many athletes believe that a particular article of clothing, a routine for getting dressed, and/or a certain pregame meal dictates the quality of their athletic prowess that day.

Illogical to most people, the belief that they can influence a computerized machine, that the machine emits feelings, or that an article of clothing dictates athletic prowess is real to some people. For these people, their beliefs influence the way they live. Perhaps you have ideas or "superstitions" that you believe influence how your life goes on a particular day. This is a common occurrence. These people are not necessarily out of touch with objective reality. While people may know, at some level, that slot machines pay according to preset, computerized odds or that athletic prowess has nothing to do with dressing routines, the belief systems continue. What dictates the behavior and beliefs discussed above or in daily "superstitions" have nothing to do with objective reality and everything to do with people's subjective reality. Subjective reality—or a person's learned definition of the situation—overrides objectivity and helps determine how people behave and/or what they believe.

While these examples may be simplistic, according to social constructionism, the same processes influence everyone—always. In practice, understanding that people's behavior does not depend on the objective existence of something, but on their subjective interpretation of it, is crucial to effective application of AMS. This knowledge is most helpful during client engagement. If practitioners remember that practice is about understanding people's perceptions and not objective reality, they reduce the likelihood that clients will feel misunderstood, there will be fewer disagreements, and it becomes easier to avoid the trap of defining normal behavior as client resistance or a diagnosable mental disorder. This perspective contributes to a professional relationship based in the client's life and belief systems, is consistent with his or her worldview, and one that is culturally appropriate for the client. Being mindful that the definitions people learn from their culture underlies not only what they do but also what they perceive, feel, and think places practitioners on the correct path to "start where the client is." Social constructionism emphasizes the cultural uniqueness of each client and/or client-system and the need to understand each client and/or client-system in her own context and belief systems, not the practitioner's context or belief systems.

Social constructionism also posits that different people attribute different meaning to the same events, because the interactional contexts and the way individuals interpret these contexts are different for everyone, even within the same family or community. One cannot assume that people raised in the same family will define their social world similarly. Individuals, in the context of their environments, derive meaning through a complex process of individual interpretation. This is how siblings from the same family can be so different, almost as if they did not grow up in the same family. For example, the sound of gunfire in the middle of the night may be frightening or normal, depending upon where a person resides and what is routine and accepted in his specific environment. Moreover, simply because some members of a family or community understand nightly gunfire as normal does not mean that others in the same family or community will feel the same.

Additionally, social constructionism examines how people construct meaning with language and established or evolving cultural beliefs. For example, alcohol consumption is defined as problematic depending upon how the concept of "alcohol problem" is socially constructed in specific environments. Clients from so-called drinking cultures may define drinking six alcoholic drinks daily as normal, while someone from a different cultural background may see this level of consumption as problematic. One of the authors worked in Russia and found an issue that demonstrates this point explicitly. Colleagues in Russia stated rather emphatically that consuming one "bottle" (approximately a U.S. pint) of vodka per day was acceptable and normal. People that consume more than one bottle per day were defined as having a drinking problem. The same level of consumption in the United States would be considered by most as clear evidence of problem drinking.

Biopsychosocial Perspective

Alone, the ecological systems perspective, even with the addition of social constructionism, does not provide the basis for the holistic understanding required by AMS. While it provides a multi-systemic lens, the ecological systems perspective focuses mostly on externals. That is, how people interact and adapt to their environments and how environments interact and adapt to people. Yet, much of what practitioners consider "clinical" focuses on "internals" or human psychological and emotional functioning. Therefore, the ecological systems perspective provides only one part of the holistic picture required by the advanced multi-systemic approach. By adding the biopsychosocial perspective, practitioners can consider the internal workings of human beings to help explain how external and internal subsystems interact.

What is the biopsychosocial perspective? It is a theoretical perspective that considers how human biological, psychological, and social-functioning subsystems interact to account for how people live in their environment. Similar to social systems, human beings are also multidimensional systems comprised of multiple subsystems constantly interacting in their environment, the human body. The biopsychosocial perspective applies multi-systemic thinking to individual human beings.

Several elements comprise the biopsychosocial perspective. Longres (2000) identifies two dimensions of individual functioning, the biophysical and the psychological; subdividing the psychological into three subdimensions: the cognitive, affective, and behavioral. Elsewhere, we added the spiritual/existential dimension to this conception (Johnson, 2004). Understanding how the biological, psychological, spiritual, existential, and social subsystems interact is instrumental in developing an appreciation of how individuals influence and are influenced by their social systemic environments. Realizing that each of these dimensions interacts with external social and environmental systems allow practitioners to enlarge their frame of reference, leading to a more holistic multi-systemic view of clients and client-systems.

Strengths/Empowerment Perspective

Over the last few years, the strengths perspective has emerged as an important part of social work theory and practice. The strengths perspective represents a significant change in how social workers conceptualize clients and client-systems. According to Saleebey (2002), it is "a versatile practice approach, relying heavily on ingenuity and creativity . . . Rather than focusing on problems, your eye turns toward possibility" (p. 1). Strengths-based practitioners believe in the power of possibility and hope in helping people overcome problems by focusing on, locating, and supporting existing personal or systemic strengths and resiliencies. The strengths perspective is based on the belief that people, regardless of the severity of their problems, have the capabilities and resources to play an active role in helping solve their own problems. The practitioner's role is to engage clients in a way that unleashes these capabilities and resources toward solving problems and changing lives.

Empowerment

Any discussion of strengths-based approaches must also consider empowerment as an instrumental element of the approach. Empowerment, as a term in social work, has evolved over the years. We choose a definition of empowerment that focuses on power; internal, interpersonal, and environmental (Parsons, Gutierrez, & Cox, 1998). According to Parsons, Gutierrez, and Cox (1998),

> In its most positive sense, power is (1) the ability to influence the course of one's life, (2) an expression of self worth, (3) the capacity to work with others to control aspects of public life, and (4) access to the mechanisms of public decision making. When used negatively, though, it can also block opportunities for stigmatized groups, exclude others and their concerns from decision making, and be a way to control others. (p. 8)

Hence, empowerment in practice is a process (Parsons, Gutierrez, and Cox, 1998) firmly grounded in ecological systems and strength-based approaches that focus on gaining power by individuals, families, groups, organizations, or communities. It is based on two related assumptions: (1) all human beings are potentially competent, even in extremely challenging situations, and (2) all human beings are subject to various degrees of powerlessness (Cox & Parsons, 1994, p. 17) and oppression (Freire, 1993). People internalize their sense of powerlessness and oppression in a way that their definition of self in the world is limited, often eliminating any notion that they can act in their own behalf in a positive manner.

An empowerment approach makes practical connections between power and powerlessness. It illuminates how these factors interact to influence clients in their daily life. Empowerment is not achieved through a single intervention, nor is it something that can be "done" to another. Empowerment does not occur through neglect or by simply giving responsibility for life and well-being to the poor or troubled, allowing them to be "free" from government regulation, support, or professional assistance. In other words, empowerment of disenfranchised groups does not occur simply by dismantling systems (such as the welfare system) to allow these groups or individuals to take responsibility for themselves. Hence, empowerment does not preclude helping.

Consistent with our definition, empowerment develops through the approach taken toward helping, not the act of helping itself. Empowerment is a sense of gained or regained power that provides the foundation for change in the short term, and stimulates a person's belief in their ability to positively influence their lives over the long term. Empowerment occurs as a function of the long-term approach of the practitioner and the professional relationship developed between practitioner and client. One cannot provide an empowering context through a constant focus on problems, deficits, inadequacies, negative labeling, and dependency.

The Power of Choice

Choice is an instrumental part of strengths-based and empowerment approaches, by recognizing that people, because of inherent strengths and capabilities, can make informed choices about their lives, just like people who are not clients. Practitioners work toward offering people choices about how they define their lives and problems, the extent to which they want to address their problems, and the means or mechanisms through which change should occur. Clients become active and instrumental partners in the helping process. They are not passive vessels, waiting for practitioners to "change them" through some crafty intervention or technique.

We are not talking about the false choices sometimes given to clients by practitioners. For example, clients with substance abuse problems are often told that they must either abstain or leave treatment. Most practitioners ignore, or use as evidence of denial, client requests to attempt so-called controlled use. If practitioners were interested in offering true choice, they would work with these clients toward their controlled-drinking goal in an effort to reduce the potential harm that may result from their use of substances (Johnson, 2004; van Wormer & Davis, 2003), even if the practitioner believes that controlled drinking is not possible. Abstinence would become the goal only when their clients choose to include it as a goal.

Client Engagement as Cultural Competence

Empowerment (choice) occurs through a process of culturally competent client engagement, created by identifying strengths, generating dialogue targeted at revealing the extent of people's oppression (Freire, 1993), and respecting their right to make informed choices in their lives. Accordingly, empowerment is the "transformation from individual and collective powerlessness to personal, political, and cultural power" (GlenMaye, 1998, p. 29), through a strengths-based relationship with a professional helper.

Successful application of AMS requires the ability to engage clients in open and trusting professional relationships. The skills needed to engage clients from different backgrounds and with different personal and cultural histories are what drive practice and what determine the difference between successful and unsuccessful practice. Advanced client engagement skills allow the practitioner to elicit in-depth, multi-systemic information in a dialogue between client and practitioner (Johnson, 2004), providing the foundation for strengths-based client empowerment leading to change.

Earlier, we defined client engagement as a mutual process occurring between clients and practitioners in a professional context, created by practitioners. In other words, creating the professional space and open atmosphere that allows engagement to flourish is the primary responsibility of the practitioner, not the client. Practitioners must have the skills and knowledge to adjust their approach toward specific clients and the client's cultural context and not *vice versa.* Clients do not adjust to us and our beliefs, values, and practices—we adjust to them. When that occurs, the foundation exists for client engagement. By definition, relationships of this nature must be performed in a culturally competent manner. Yet, what does this mean?

Over the last two decades, social work and other helping professions have been concerned with cultural competence in practice (Fong, 2001). Beginning in the late 1970s, the professional literature has been replete with ideas, definitions, and practice models designed to increase cultural awareness and promote culturally appropriate practice methods. Yet, despite the attention given to the issue, there remains confusion about how to define and teach culturally competent practice.

Structural and Historical Systems of Oppression: Who Holds the Power?

Often embedded in laws, policies, and social institutions are oppressive influences such as racism, sexism, homophobia, and classism, to name a few. These structural issues play a significant role in the lives of clients (through maltreatment and discrimination) and in social work practice. How people are treated (or how they internalize historical treatment of self, family, friends, and/or ancestors) shapes how they believe, think, and act in the present. Oppression affects how they perceive that others feel about them, how they view the world and their place in it, and how receptive they are to professional service providers. Therefore, culturally competent practice must consider the impact of structural systems of oppression and injustice on clients, their problems, strengths, and potential for change.

Oppression is a by-product of socially constructed notions of power, privilege, control, and hierarchies of difference. As stated above, it is created and maintained by differences in power. By definition, those who have power can force people to abide by the rules, standards, and actions the powerful deem worthwhile, mandatory, or acceptable. Those who hold power can enforce particular worldviews; deny equal access and opportunity to housing, employment, or health care; define right and wrong, normal and abnormal; and imprison, confine, and/or commit physical, emotional, or mental violence against the powerless (McLaren, 1995; Freire, 1993). Most importantly, power permits the holder to "set the very terms of power" (Appleby, 2001, p. 37). It defines the interaction between the oppressed and the oppressor, and between the social worker and client.

Social institutions and practices are developed and maintained by the dominant culture to meet *its* needs and maintain *its* power. Everything and everybody is judged and classified accordingly. Even when the majority culture develops programs or engages in helping activities, these efforts will not include measures that threaten the dominant group's position at the top of the social hierarchy (Freire, 1993). For example, Kozol (1991) wrote eloquently about how public schools fail by design, while Freire (1993) wrote about how state welfare and private charity provide short-term assistance while ensuring that there are not enough resources to lift people permanently out of poverty.

Oppression is neither an academic nor a theoretical consideration; it is not a faded relic of a bygone era. Racism did not end with the civil rights movement, and sexism was not eradicated by the feminist movement. Understanding how systems of oppression work in people's lives is of paramount importance for every individual and family seeking professional help, including those who belong to the *same* race, gender, and class as the practitioner. No two individuals, regardless of their personal demographics, experience the world in the same way. Often, clients are treated ineffectively by professional helpers who mistakenly believe that people who look or act the same will experience the world in similar ways. These workers base their assumptions about clients on stereotypic descriptions of culture, lifestyle, beliefs, and practices. They take group-level data (i.e., many African American adolescents join gangs because of broken families and poverty) and assume that *all* African American teenagers are gang members from single-parent families. Social work values and ethics demand a higher standard, one that compels us to go beyond stereotypes. Our job is to discover, understand, and utilize personal differences in the assessment and treatment process to benefit clients, not use differences as a way of limiting clients' potential for health and well-being.

We cannot accurately assess or treat people without considering the effects of oppression related to race, ethnicity, culture, sexual preference, gender, or physical/emotional status. We need to understand how oppression influences our clients' beliefs about problems and potential approaches to problem solving, and how it determines what kind of support they can expect to receive if they decide to seek help. For example, despite the widely held belief that chemical dependency is an equal opportunity disease (Gordon, 1993), it is clear that some people are more vulnerable than others. While some of the general themes of chemical dependency may appear universal, each client is unique. That is, an individual's dependency results from personal behavior, culture (including the history of one's culture), past experiences, and family interacting with larger social systems that provide opportunities or impose limits on the individual (Johnson, 2000).

Systems of oppression ensure unequal access to resources for certain individuals, families, and communities. However, while all oppressed people are similar in that they lack the power to define their place in the social hierarchy, oppression based on race, gender, sexual orientation, class, and other social factors is expressed in a variety of ways. Learning about cultural nuances is important in client assessment, treatment planning, and treatment (Lum, 1999). According to Pinderhughes (1989), there is no such thing as culture-free service delivery. Cultural differences between clients and social workers in terms of values, norms, beliefs, attitudes, lifestyles, and life opportunities affect every aspect of practice.

What Is Culture?

Many different concepts of culture are used in social work, sociology, and anthropology. Smelser (1992) considers culture a "system of patterned values, meanings, and beliefs that give cognitive structure to the world, provide a basis for coordinating and controlling human interactions, and constitute a link as the system is transmitted from one generation to another" (p. 11). Geertz (1973) regarded culture as simultaneously a product of and a guide to people searching for organized categories and interpretations that provide a meaningful experiential link to their social life. Building upon these two ideas, in this book we abide by the following definition of culture proposed elsewhere (Johnson, 2000):

> Culture is historical, bound up in traditions and practices passed through generations; memories of events—real or imagined—that define a people and their worldview. (Culture) is viewed as collective subjectivity, or a way of life adopted by a community that ultimately defines their worldview. (p. 121)

Consistent with this definition, the collective subjectivities called culture are pervasive forces in the way people interact, believe, think, feel, and act in their social world. Culture plays a significant role in shaping how people view the world. As a historical force, in part built on ideas, definitions, and events passed through generations, culture also defines people's level of social acceptance by the wider community; shapes how people live, think, and act; and influences how people perceive that others feel about them and how they view the world and their place in it. Thus, it is impossible to understand a client without grasping his or her cultural foundations.

Cultural Competence

As stated earlier, over the years many different ideas and definitions of what constitutes culturally competent practice have developed, as indicated by the growth of the professional literature since the late 1970s. To date, focus has primarily been placed in two areas: (1) the need for practitioners to be aware or their own cultural beliefs, ideas, and identities leading to cultural sensitivity, and (2) learning factual and descriptive information about various ethnic and racial groups based mostly on group-level survey data and analyses. Fong (2001) suggests that culture is often considered "tangential" to individual functioning and is not central to the client's functioning (p. 5).

To address this issue, Fong (2001) builds on Lum's (1999) culturally competent practice model that focuses on four areas: (1) cultural awareness, (2) knowledge acquisition, (3) skill development, and (4) inductive learning. Besides inductive learning, Lum's model places focuses mainly on practitioners in perpetual self-awareness, gaining knowledge about cultures, and skill building. While these are important ideas for cultural competence, Fong (2001) calls for a shift in thinking and practice, "to provide a culturally competent service focused solely on the client rather than the social worker and what he or she brings to the awareness of ethnicity" (p. 5). Fong (2001) suggests an "extension" (p. 6) of Lum's model by turning the focus of each of the four elements away from the practitioner toward the client. For example, cultural awareness changes from a practitioner focus to "the social worker's understanding and the identification of the critical cultural values important to the client system and to themselves" (p. 6). This change allows Fong (2001) to remain consistent with the stated definition of culturally competent practice, insisting that practitioners,

> . . . operating from an empowerment, strengths, and ecological framework, provide services, conduct assessments, and implement interventions that are reflective of the clients' cultural values and norms, congruent with their natural help-seeking behaviors, and inclusive of existing indigenous solutions. (p. 1)

While we agree with the idea that "to be culturally competent is to know the cultural values of the client-system and to use them in planning and implementing services" (Fong, 2001, p. 6), we want to make this shift the main point of a culturally competent model of client engagement. That is, beyond what should or must occur, we believe that professional education and training must focus on the skills of culturally competent client engagement that are necessary to make this happen. This model places individual client cultural information at the center of practice. We agree with Fong (2001) that having culturally sensitive or culturally aware practitioners is not nearly enough. Practitioner self-awareness and knowledge of different cultures does not constitute cultural competence. We strive to find a method for reaching this worthy goal.

The central issue revolves around practitioners participating in inductive learning and the skills of grounded theory. In other words, regardless of practitioner beliefs, awarenesses, or sensitivities, their job is to learn about and understand their client's world, and "ground" their theory of practice in the cultural context of their client. They develop a unique theory of human behavior in a multi-systemic context for every client. Culturally competent client engagement does not happen by assessing the extent to which client lives "fit" within existing theory and knowledge about reality, most of which is middle-class and Eurocentric at its core. Cultural competence (Johnson, 2004)

> . . . *begins* with learning about different cultures, races, personal circumstances, and structural mechanisms of oppression. It *occurs* when practitioners master the interpersonal skills needed to move beyond general descriptions of a specific culture or race to learn specific individual, family, group, or community interpretations of culture, ethnicity, and race. The culturally competent practitioner knows that within each culture are individually interpreted and practiced thoughts, beliefs, and behaviors that may or may not be consistent with group-level information. That is, there is tremendous diversity within groups, as well as between them. Individuals are unique unto themselves, not simply interchangeable members of a specific culture, ethnicity, or race who natu-

> rally abide by the group-level norms often taught on graduate and undergraduate courses on human diversity. (p. 105)

Culturally competent client engagement revolves around the practitioner's ability to create a relationship, through the professional use of self, based in true dialogue (Freire, 1993; Johnson, 2004). We define dialogue as "a joint endeavor, developed between people (in this case, practitioner and client) that move clients from their current state of hopelessness to a more hopeful, motivated position in their world" (Johnson, 2004, p. 97). Elsewhere (Johnson, 2004), we detailed a model of culturally competent engagement based on Freire's (1993) definitions of oppression, communication, dialogue, practitioner self-work, and the ability to exhibit worldview respect, hope, humility, trust, and empathy.

To investigate culture in a competent manner is to take a comprehensive look into people's worldviews—to discover what they believe about the world and their place in it. It goes beyond race and ethnicity (although these are important issues) into how culture determines thoughts, feelings, and behaviors in daily life. This includes what culture says about people's problems; culturally appropriate strengths and resources; the impact of gender on these issues; and what it means to seek professional help (Leigh, 1998).

The larger questions to be answered are how clients uniquely and individually interpret their culture; how their beliefs, attitudes, and behaviors are shaped by that interpretation, and how these cultural beliefs and practices affect daily life and determine lifestyle in the context of the larger community. Additionally, based on their cultural membership, beliefs, and practices, practitioners need to discover the potential and real barriers faced by clients in the world. Many clients, because they are part of non-majority cultures, face issues generated by social systems of oppression such as racism, sexism, homophobia, and ethnocentrism that expose them to limitations and barriers that others do not face.

What is the value of culturally competent client engagement? Helping clients discuss their attitudes, beliefs, and behaviors in the context of their culture—including their religious or spiritual belief systems—offers valuable information about their worldview, sense of social and spiritual connection, and/or practical involvement in their social world. Moreover, establishing connections between their unique interpretation of their culture and their daily life provides vital clues about people's belief systems, attitudes, expectations (social construction of reality), and explanation of behaviors that cannot be understood outside the context of their socially constructed interpretation of culture.

A Cautionary Note

It is easy to remember to ask about culture when clients are obviously different (i.e., different races, countries of origin, etc.). However, many practitioners forgo cultural investigation with clients they consider to have the same cultural background as the practitioner. For example, the search for differences between European

Americans with Christian beliefs—if the social worker shares these characteristics—gets lost in mutual assumptions, based on the misguided belief that there are no important differences between them. The same is often true when clients and practitioners come from the same racial, cultural, or lifestyle backgrounds (i.e., African American practitioner and client, gay practitioner and gay client, etc.). Culturally competent practice means that practitioners are always interested in people's individual interpretation of their culture and their subjective definitions of reality, whether potential differences are readily apparent or not. Practitioners must be diligent to explore culture with clients who appear to be from the same background as the practitioner, just as they would with people who are obviously from different cultural, racial, ethnic, or religious backgrounds.

Multiple Theories and Methods

No single theory, model, or method is best suited to meet the needs of all clients (Miley, O'Melia, & DuBois, 2004). Consistent with this statement, one of the hallmarks of AMS is the expectation that practitioners must determine which theory, model, or method will best suit a particular client. Choosing from a range of approaches and interventions, AMS practitioners develop the skills and abilities to: (1) determine, based on the client's life, history, culture, and style, which treatment approach (theory and/or method) would best suit their needs and achieve the desired outcome, (2) determine which modality or modalities (individual, family, group treatment, etc.) will best meet the need of their clients, and (3) conduct treatment according to their informed clinical decisions.

Over the last 20 years or so, graduate social work education has trended toward practice specialization through concentration-based curricula. Many graduate schools of social work build on the generalist foundation by insisting that students focus on learning specific practice models or theories (disease, cognitive-behavioral, psychoanalysis, etc.) and/or specific practice methods (individual, family, group, etc.), often at the exclusion of other methods or models. For example, students often enter the field intent on doing therapy with individuals, say, from a cognitive-behavioral approach only.

This trend encourages practitioners to believe that one approach or theory best represents the "Truth." Truth, in this sense, is the belief that one theory or approach works best for most people, most of the time. It helps create a practice scenario that leads practitioners to use their chosen approach with every client they treat. Therefore, practice becomes a process of the practitioner forcing clients to adjust to the practitioner's beliefs and expectations about the nature of problems, the course of treatment, and definition of positive versus negative outcomes. From this perspective, what is best for clients is determined by what the practitioner believes is best, not what clients believe is in their best interest.

Some practitioners take their belief in the Truth of a particular theory or method to extremes. They believe that one model or theory works best for all people, all the time. We found this to be common in the family therapy field, whereby some true believers insist that everyone needs family therapy—so that is all they offer. What's worse is that many of these same practitioners know and use only one particular family therapy theory and model. The "true believer" approach can cause problems, especially for clients. For example, when clients do not respond to treatment, instead of looking to other approaches, true believers simply prescribe more of the method that did not work in the first place. If a more intensive application of the method does not work, then the client's "lack of readiness" for treatment, resistance, or denial becomes the culprit. These practitioners usually give little thought to their practice approach or personal style and its impact on client "readiness" for treatment. They fail to examine the role their personal style, beliefs, attitudes, and practices have in creating the context that led to clients not succeeding in treatment.

Each practice theory and model has a relatively unique way of defining client problems, practitioner method and approach, interventions, and what constitutes successful outcome. For practitioners to believe that one theory or model is true, even if only for most people, they must believe in the universality of problems, methods and approaches, interventions, and successful outcome criteria. This contradicts the definition of theory. While being far from a concrete representation of the truth, a theory is a set of myths, expectations, guesses, and conjectures about what might be true (Best & Kellner, 1991). A theory is hypothetical; a set of ideas and explanations that need proving. No single theory can explain everything. According to Popper (1994), a theory ". . . always remains guesswork, and there is no theory that is not beset with problems" (p. 157). As such, treatment specialization can—although not always—encourage people to believe they have found the Truth where little truth exists.

Practitioners using an AMS perspective come to believe that some element of every established practice model, method, or theory may be helpful. Accordingly, every model, method, or theory can be adapted and used in a multi-systemic practice framework. As an AMS practitioner, one neither accepts any single model fully, nor disregards a model entirely if there is potential for helping a client succeed in a way that is compatible with professional social work values and ethics. These practitioners hone their critical thinking skills (Gambrill, 1997, 1990) and apply them in practice, particularly as it pertains to treatment theories, models, and methods. In the context of evidence-based practice (Cournoyer, 2004; Gibbs, 2003), sharpened critical thinking skills allow practitioners to closely read and evaluate practice theories, research, or case reports to recognize the strengths, weakness, and contradictions in theories, models, and/or policy related to social work practice.

Informed Eclecticism

The goal of AMS is for practitioners to develop an approach we call *informed eclecticism.* Informed eclecticism allows the use of multiple methods, interventions, and approaches in the context of practice that: (1) is held together by a perspective or approach that provides consistency, that makes practice choices in a way that makes sense in a particular client's life; and (2) is based, whenever possible, on the latest evidence about its efficacy with particular problems and particular clients. While it is often best to rely on empirical evidence, this data is in its infancy. AMS does not preclude the use of informed practice wisdom and personal creativity in developing intervention plans and approaches. It is up to practitioners to ensure that any treatment based in practice wisdom or that is creatively generated be discussed with colleagues, supervisors, or consultants to ensure theoretical consistency and that it fits within the code of professional ethics.

Informed eclecticism is different from the routine definition of eclecticism—the use of whatever theory, model, or method works best for their clients. While this is the goal of AMS practice specifically and social work practice in general (Timberlake, Farber, & Sabatino, 2002), it is an elusive goal indeed. Informed eclecticism often gets lost in a practitioner's quest to find something that "works." According to Gambrill (1997), eclecticism is "the view that we should adopt whatever theories or methodologies is useful in inquiry, no matter what their source and without worry about their consistency" (p. 93). The most important word in Gambrill's statement is "consistency." While there are practitioners who have managed to develop a consistent, organized, and holistic version of informed eclecticism, this is not the norm.

Too often, uninformed eclecticism resembles the following. A practitioner specializes by modality (individual therapy) and uses a variety of modality-specific ideas and practices in his work with clients; changing ideas and tactics when the approach he normally uses does not "work." This often leaves the practitioner searching (mostly in vain) for the magic intervention—what "works." Moreover, while uninformed eclectic practitioners use interventions from various "schools," they remain primarily wedded to one modality. Hence, they end up confusing themselves and their clients as they search for the "right" approach. They rarely look beyond their chosen modality and, therefore, never actually look outside of their self-imposed, theoretical cage.

For example, an uninformed eclectic practitioner specializing in individual therapy may try a cognitive approach, a client-centered approach, a Freudian approach, or a behavioral approach. A family therapy specialist may use a structural, strategic, or solution-focused approach. However, in the end, little changes. These practitioners still believe that their clients need individual or family treatment. They rarely consider potentially useful ideas and tactics taken from different modalities that could be used instead of, or in combination with, an individual or family approach, mostly because they base treatment decisions on their chosen modality.

While informed eclecticism is the goal, most find it difficult to find consistency when trying to work from a variety of models at the same time. The informed eclectic practitioners, through experience and empirical evidence, have a unifying approach that serves as the basis for using different models or methods. What is important, according to clinical outcome research, is the consistency of approach in helping facilitate successful client outcome (Gaston, 1990; Miller & Rollnick, 2002; Harper & Lantz, 1996). Trying to be eclectic makes consistency (and treatment success), quite difficult.

What uninformed eclecticism lacks is the framework needed to gain a holistic and comprehensive understanding of the client in the context of his or her life, history, and multiple environments that leads naturally to culturally consistent treatment and intervention decisions. AMS, as it is described here, provides such a framework. It is holistic, integrative, ecological, and based in the latest empirical evidence. It is an inclusive framework that bases treatment decisions on a multi-systemic assessment of specific client history and culture. It is designed, whenever possible, to capitalize on client strengths, be consistent with culturally specific help-seeking behavior, and utilize existing or formulated community-based and/or natural support systems in the client's environment.

Defining Multi-Systemic Client Information

In this section we specifically discuss the different dimensions that comprise AMS practice. This is a general look at what constitutes multi-systemic client life information. There are six levels of information that, when integrated into a life history of clients, demonstrates how multiple theories, models, and approaches can be applied to better understand, assess, and treat clients or client-systems. Generally, the six dimensions (biological, psychological, family, religious/spiritual/existential, social/environmental, and macro) encompass range of information needed to complete a comprehensive, multi-systemic assessment, treatment, and intervention plan with client-systems of all sizes and configurations.

1. Biological Dimension

AMS practitioners need to understand what some have called the "mind-body connection," or the links between social/emotional, behavioral, and potential biological or genetic issues that may be, at least in part, driving the problems presented by clients in practice. As scientific evidence mounts regarding the biological and genetic sources of personal troubles (i.e., some mental illness, etc.), it grows imperative for well-trained AMS practitioners to apply this knowledge in everyday work with clients (Ginsberg, Nackerud, & Larrison, 2004). The responsibility for understanding biology and physical health goes well beyond those working in direct healthcare practice settings (i.e., hospital, HIV, or hospice practice settings). Issues pertaining to physical health confront practitioners in all practice settings.

For example, practitioners working in mental health settings are confronted daily with issues pertaining to human biology; the sources and determinants of mental illness, differential uses of psychotropic medication, and often, the role played in client behavior by proper nutrition, appropriate health care, and even physical rest. In foster care and/or family preservation, practitioners also confront the effects of parental abuses (i.e., fetal alcohol syndrome [FAS]), medication management, and child/adolescent physical and biological development issues.

Beyond learning about the potential biological or physical determinants of various client troubles, having a keen understanding of the potential physical and health risks associated with various behaviors and/or lifestyles places practitioners in the position of intervening to save lives. For example, practitioners working with substance abusing or chemically dependent clients must understand drug pharmacology—especially drug-mixing—to predict potentially life-threatening physical withdrawal effects and/or to prevent intentional or unintentional harm caused by drug overdose (Johnson, 2004).

AMS requires that practitioners keep current with the latest information about human biology, development, genetics, and potential associated health risks facing clients and client-systems in practice. With that knowledge, practitioners can include this information during client assessment, treatment planning, and intervention strategies. It also requires practitioners to know the limits of professional responsibility. That is, social workers are not physicians and should never offer medical advice or guidance that is not supported by properly trained physicians. Therefore, AMS practitioners utilize the appropriate medical professionals as part of assessment, planning, and intervention processes with all clients.

2. Psychological/Emotional Dimension

AMS practitioners need a working knowledge of the ways that psychological and emotional functioning are intertwined with clients' problems and strengths, how issues from this dimension contribute to the way their client or client-system interacts with self and others in their environment, and how their environments influence their psychological and emotional functioning. There are several important skill sets that practitioners must develop to consider issues in this dimension. First, being able to recognize potential problems through a mental screening examination is a skill necessary to all practitioners. Also, having a keen understanding of the *Diagnostic and Statistical Manual of Mental Disorders* (DSM) (American Psychological Association, 2000), including the multi-axial diagnostic process, and recognition of the limits of this tool in the overall multi-systemic assessment process is instrumental. Especially critical is the ability to recognize co-occurring disorders (Johnson, 2004). It is also valuable to learn the Person-in-Environment (PIE) assessment system (Karls & Wandrei, 1994a, 1994b), a diagnostic model developed specifically for social workers to incorporate environmental influences.

In addition to understanding how psychology and emotion affects client mood and behavior, AMS practitioners also know how to employ different theories and models used for treating psychological and emotional functioning problems in the context of a client's multi-systemic assessment and treatment plan. This includes methods of treating individuals, families, and groups. Depending on the client's multi-systemic assessment, each of these modalities or some combination of modalities is appropriate for people with problems in this dimension.

3. Family Dimension

The family is the primary source of socialization, modeling, and nurturing of children. Hence, the family system has a significant impact on people's behavior, and people's behavior has significant impact on the health and well-being of their family system (Johnson, 2004). By integrating a family systems perspective into AMS, practitioners will often be able to make sense of behavior attitudes, beliefs, and values that would otherwise be difficult to understand or explain.

For our purposes, a family is defined as a group of people—regardless of their actual blood or legal relationship—whom clients consider to be members of their family (Johnson, 2004). This definition is designed to privilege clients' perceptions and subjective construction of reality and avoid disagreements over who is or is not in someone's family. So, if a client refers to a neighbor as "Uncle Joe," then that perception represents their reality. What good would it do to argue otherwise? Just as in client engagement discussed earlier, AMS practitioners seek to understand and embrace their client's unique definition of family, rather than imposing a rigid standard that may not fit their perceived reality. This is especially important when dealing with gay and lesbian clients. The law may not recognize gay or lesbian marriage, but AMS practitioners must, if that is the nature of the client's relationship and consistent with their belief system.

It is important to have a working knowledge of different theories and approaches to assessing and treating families and couples, as well as the ability to construct three-generation genograms to help conceptualize family systems and characterize the relationships that exist within the family system and between the family and its environment. Family treatment requires unique skills, specialized post-graduate training, and regular supervision before a practitioner can master the methods and call herself a "family therapist." However, the journey toward mastery is well worth it. Family treatment can be among the most effective and meaningful treatment modalities, often used in conjunction with other modalities (individual and/or group treatment), or as the primary treatment method.

4. Religious/Spiritual/Existential Dimension

Practitioners, students, and social work educators are often wary of exploring issues related to religion and spirituality in practice or the classroom. While there are exceptions, this important dimension often goes unexamined. Exploring people's religious beliefs and/or the tenets of their faith, even if they do not appear to have faith or spiritual beliefs, as they pertain to people's subjective definition of self in relation to the world is an important part of AMS practice.

How clients view themselves in relation to others and their world provides an interesting window into the inner workings of their individual interpretation of culture. The extent that clients have internalized messages (positive, negative, and/or neutral) about their behavior from their faith community or personal spiritual belief systems can lead to an understanding of why people approach their lives and others in the ways they do. Moreover, much can be learned, based on these beliefs, about people's belief in the potential for change, how change occurs, and whom is best suited to help in that change process (if anyone at all), especially as it relates to the many moral and religious messages conveyed about people with problems.

Examination of this dimension goes beyond discovering which church or synagogue clients attend. It is designed to learn how and by what means clients define themselves and their lives in their worlds. What tenets they use to justify their lives, and how these tenets either support their current lives or not can be used to help lead them toward change. There is much to be learned about client culture, how people interpret their culture in daily life, and how they view their life in their personal context from an examination of their religious or spiritual beliefs.

Moreover, religious and spiritual belief systems can also be a source of strength and support when considered in treatment plans. For example, while many clients may benefit from attendance at a community support group (i.e., Alcoholics Anonymous, Overeaters Anonymous, etc.) or professional treatment, some will benefit even more from participation in groups and events through local houses of worship. In our experience, many clients unable to succeed in professional treatment or support groups found success through a connection or reconnection with organizations that share their faith, whatever that faith may be.

5. Social/Environmental Dimension

Beyond the individual and family, AMS practitioners look to the client's community, including the physical environment, for important clues to help with engagement, assessment, and intervention planning. People live in communities comprised of three different types: (1) location (neighborhoods, cities, and rural or urban villages), (2) identification (religion, culture, race, etc.), and (3) affiliation (group memberships, subcultures, professional, political/ideological groups, etc.). There are five subdimensions that comprise the social/environmental dimension and incorporate the three types of communities listed above (Johnson, 2004):

1. Local community. This includes learning about physical environment, living conditions, a person's fit within her community, neighborhoods, where and how people live on a daily basis, and how they believe they are treated and/or accepted by community members and the community's power structure (i.e., the police, etc.).

2. Cultural context. This includes learning about clients' larger culture, their individual interpretation of culture, and how it drives or influences their daily life. Also included here is an exploration of histories of oppression and discrimination (individual, family, and community) and a client's subcultural group membership (i.e., drug culture, gang culture, etc.).

3. Social class. Often overlooked by practitioners, "information about people's social class is directly related to information about their families, the goodness-of-fit between the person and environment, and the strengths, resources, and/or barriers in their communities" (Johnson, 2004, p. 226). Some believe that no other demographic factor explains so extensively the differences between people and/or groups (Lipsitz, 1997; Davis & Proctor, 1989). Social class represents a combination of income, education, occupation, prestige, and community. It encompasses how these factors affect people's relative wealth and access to power and opportunity (Johnson, 2004).

4. Social/relational. Human beings are social creatures who define themselves in relation to others (Johnson, 2004). Therefore, it is necessary to know something about people's ability to relate to others in their social environment. This investigation includes loved ones, friends, peers, supervisors, teachers, and others that they relate to in their daily life.

5. Legal history and involvement. Obviously, this subdimension includes information about involvement with the legal system, by the client, family members, and friends and peers. More than recording a simple demographic history, seek to discover their feelings, attitudes, and beliefs about themselves, their place in the world, and how their brushes with the law fit into or influence their worldview.

6. Community resources. Investigate the nature and availability of organizational support, including the role of social service organizations, politics, and your presence as a social worker in a client's life. For example, can clients find a program to serve their needs, or what does seeing a social worker mean within their community or culture? What are the conditions of the schools and the influence of churches, neighborhood associations, and block clubs? More importantly, what is the prevailing culture of the local environment? Are neighbors supportive or afraid of each other, and can a client expect to reside in the present situation and receive the support needed to change?

Be sure to include the professional helping system in this subdimension. Practitioners, their agencies, and the policies that assist or impede the professional helping process join with client-systems as part of the overall system in treatment. In other words, we must consider ourselves as part of the system—we do not stand outside in objective observation. This includes practitioner qualities and styles, agency policies, broader policies related to specific populations, and reimbursement policies, including managed care. All of these factors routinely influence the extent to which clients receive help, how clients are perceived in the helping system and, in the case of reimbursement policies, the method of treatment clients are eligible to receive regardless of how their multi-systemic assessment turns out.

Familiarity with various theories and models of community provide the keys to understanding the role of the social, physical, political, and economic environment in an individual's life. Community models look at the broader environment and its impact on people. Clients or client-systems with issues located in this dimension often respond well to group and family treatment methods. Occasionally, practitioners will be required to intervene at the local neighborhood or community level through organizing efforts and/or personal or political advocacy. For example:

> I (Johnson) was treating a client in individual and occasional family treatment when it was discovered that the daughter had been molested by a neighbor. The parents had not reported the molestation. I soon learned that this neighbor was rumored to have molested several young girls in the neighborhood and that nobody was willing to

report the molestations. I urged my client to organize a neighborhood meeting of all involved parents at her home. I served as the group facilitator for an intense meeting that ultimately built the community support needed to involve law enforcement. Within days, all of the parents in this group met with law enforcement. The perpetrator was arrested, convicted, and sentenced to life imprisonment.

6. Macro Dimension

AMS practitioners do not stop looking for relevant client information at the local level. They also look for clues in the way that macro issues influence clients, their problems, and potential for change. Knowledge of various laws (local, state, and national) are critical, as well as an understanding of how various social policies are interpreted and enforced in a particular client's life. For example, AMS requires an understanding of how child welfare policies affect the life of a chemically dependent mother, how healthcare policy affects a family's decisions about seeking medical treatment for their children, or how local standards of hygiene or cleanliness affect a family's status and acceptance in their community.

Issues to consider at this level also include public sentiment, stereotypes, and mechanisms of oppression that play a significant role in the lives of people who are not Caucasian, male, middle-class (or more affluent) citizens. Racism, classism, homophobia, and sexism, to name a few, are real threats to people who are attempting to live a "normal" life. An AMS practitioner must understand this reality and learn from clients what their individual perceptions are of these mechanisms and how they affect their problems and potential for change. The macro dimension involves issues such as housing, employment, and public support, along with the dynamics of the criminal justice system. For example, if clients have been arrested for domestic violence, what is the chance they will get fair and just legal representation? If they have been convicted and served jail or prison sentences, what are the chances they will have a reasonable chance of finding sufficient employment upon release?

These issues can be addressed in individual, family, or group treatments. Often, group treatment is an effective way to address issues clients struggle with at the macro level. Group treatment provides clients with a way to address these issues in the context of mutual social support and a sense of belonging, helping them realize that they are not alone in their struggles (Yalom, 1995). AMS practitioners also recognize the need for political advocacy and community organizing methods for clients who present with consistent struggles with issues at the macro level.

Summary

The hallmark of AMS is its reliance on and integration of multi-systemic client information into one comprehensive assessment, treatment, and intervention plan. It incorporates knowledge, skills, and values from multiple sources, and relies on various sources of knowledge to paint a holistic picture of people's lives, struggles, strengths and resources, and potentials for change. Practitioners need a current working knowledge of human behavior, social systems theories, the latest social research and practice evaluation results, the impact of public laws and policies, as well as the skills and abilities to plan and implement treatment approaches as needed, in a manner consistent with our definition of informed eclecticism.

Many students new to AMS start out confused because the requirements seem so diverse and complicated. However, as you will see in the case presentations to follow, an organized and efficient practitioner who has learned to think and act multi-systemically can gather large amounts of critically important information about a client in a relatively short period. For this to happen, you must have a deep understanding of various theories, models, and practice approaches that address the various systemic levels considered and be willing to accept that no single model is completely right or wrong. It is always easier to latch on to one model and "go with it." However, the goal of practice is not to be correct or to promote your own ease and comfort, but to develop an assessment and treatment plan that is right for each client, whether or not you would ever use it in your own life. Social work practice is not about the social worker, but the client. It is important never to lose sight of this fact.

Bibliography

American Psychiatric Association (2000). *Diagnostic and statistical manual of mental disorders* (4th ed., TR). Washington, DC: Author.

Appleby, G. A. (2001). Dynamics of oppression and discrimination. In G. A. Appleby, E. Colon, & J. Hamilton (eds.), *Diversity, oppression, and social functioning: Person-in-environment assessment and intervention.* Boston: Allyn and Bacon.

Best, S., & Kellner, D. (1991). *Postmodern theory: Critical interrogations.* New York: Guilford Press.

Cournoyer, B. R. (2004). *The evidence-based social work skills book.* Boston: Allyn and Bacon.

Cox, E. O., & Parsons, R. J. (1994). *Empowerment-oriented social work practice with the elderly.* Pacific Grove, CA: Brooks/Cole.

Davis, L. E., & Proctor, E. K. (1989). *Race, gender, and class: Guidelines for practice with individuals, families, and groups.* Englewood Cliffs, NJ: Prentice-Hall.

Derezotes, D. S. (2000). *Advanced generalist social work practice.* Thousand Oaks, CA: Sage.

Fong, R. (2001). Culturally competent social work practice: Past and present. In R. Fong & S. Furuto (eds.), *Culturally competent practice: Skills, interventions, and evaluations.* Boston: Allyn and Bacon.

Freire, P. (1993). *Pedagogy of the oppressed.* New York: Continuum.

Gambrill, E. (1997). *Social work practice: A critical thinker's guide.* New York: Oxford University Press.

Gambrill, E. (1990). *Critical thinking in clinical practice.* San Francisco: Jossey-Bass.

Gaston, L. (1990). The concept of the alliance and its role in psychotherapy: Theoretical and empirical considerations. *Psychotherapy, 27,* 143–153.

Geertz, C. (1973). *The interpretation of cultures.* New York: Basic Books.

Germain, C. B., & Gitterman, A. (1996). *The life model of social work practice* (2nd ed.). New York: Columbia University Press.

Germain, C. B., & Gitterman, A. (1980). *The ecological model of social work practice.* New York: Columbia University Press.

Gibbs, L. E. (2003). *Evidence-based practice for the helping professions: A practical guide with integrated multimedia.* Pacific Grove, CA: Brooks/Cole.

Ginsberg, L., Nackerud, L., & Larrison, C. R. (2004). *Human biology for social workers: Development, ecology, genetics, and health.* Boston: Allyn and Bacon.

GlenMaye, L. (1998). Empowerment of women. In L. M. Gutierrez, R. J. Parsons, & E. O. Cox (eds.), *Empowerment in social work practice: A sourcebook.* Pacific Grove, CA: Brooks/Cole.

Gordon, J. U. (1993). A culturally specific approach to ethnic minority young adults. In E. M. Freeman (ed.), *Substance abuse treatment: A family systems perspective.* Newbury Park, CA: Sage.

Greif, G. L. (1986). The ecosystems perspective "meets the press." *Social Work, 31,* 225–226.

Harper, K. V., & Lantz, J. (1996). *Cross-cultural practice: Social work practice with diverse populations.* Chicago: Lyceum Books.

Johnson, J. L. (2004). *Fundamentals of substance abuse practice.* Pacific Grove, CA: Brooks/Cole.

Johnson, J. L. (2000). *Crossing borders—Confronting history: Intercultural adjustment in a post-Cold War world.* Lanham, MD: University Press of America.

Karls, J., & Wandrei, K. (1994a). *Person-in-environment system: The PIE classification system for functioning problems.* Washington, DC: NASW.

Karls, J., & Wandrei, K. (1994b). *PIE manual: Person-in-environment system: The PIE classification system for social functioning.* Washington, DC: NASW.

Kozol, J. (1991). *Savage inequalities: Children in America's schools.* New York: Crown Publishers.

Leigh, J. W. (1998). *Communicating for cultural competence.* Boston: Allyn and Bacon.

Lipsitz, G. (1997). Class and class consciousness: Teaching about social class in public universities. In A. Kumar (ed.), *Class issues.* New York: New York University Press.

Longres, J. F. (2000). *Human behavior in the social environment* (3rd ed.). Itasca, IL: F. E. Peacock.

Lum, D. (1999). *Culturally competent practice.* Pacific Grove, CA: Brooks/Cole.

McLaren, P. (1995). *Critical pedagogy and predatory culture: Oppositional politics in a postmodern era.* London: Routledge.

Miley, K. K., O'Melia, M., & DuBois, B. (2004). *Generalist social work practice: An empowerment approach.* Boston: Allyn and Bacon.

Miller, W. R., & Rollnick, S. (2002). *Motivational interviewing: Preparing people to change addictive behavior* (2nd ed.). New York: Guilford Press.

Mills, C. W. (1959). *The sociological imagination.* New York: Oxford University Press.

Parsons, R. J., Gutierrez, L. M., & Cox, E. O. (1998). A model for empowerment practice. In L. M. Gutierrez, R. J. Parsons, & E. O. Cox (eds.), *Empowerment in social work practice: A sourcebook.* Pacific Grove, CA: Brooks/Cole.

Pinderhughes, E. (1989). *Understanding race, ethnicity, and power.* New York: Free Press.

Popper, K. R. (1994). *The myth of the framework: In defense of science and rationality.* Edited by M. A. Notturno. New York: Routledge.

Saleebey, D. (2002). *The strengths perspective in social work practice* (3rd ed.). Boston: Allyn and Bacon.

Smelser, N. J. (1992). Culture: Coherent or incoherent. In R. Munch & N. J. Smelser (eds.), *Theory of culture.* Berkeley, CA: University of California Press.

Timberlake, E. M., Farber, M. Z., & Sabatino, C. A. (2002). *The general method of social work practice: McMahon's generalist perspective* (4th ed.). Boston: Allyn and Bacon.

van Wormer, K., & Davis, D. R. (2003). *Addiction treatment: A strengths perspective.* Pacific Grove, CA: Brooks/Cole.

Yalom, I. (1995). *The theory and practice of group psychotherapy* (4th ed.). New York: Basic Books.

2

Sarah and Robert

George Grant, Jr.

Introduction

This case addresses the issue of sibling splits in the special needs adoption, child welfare system. For those unsure about the subject, sibling splits occur when the child welfare system places siblings in different families. As you read this case, I ask you to decide if you believe, given all the evidence, a sibling split should occur. I also ask you to support the reasons for your decision in the context of the professional literature, practice experience, and/or dialogue with classmates. Finally, I ask you to examine your community to discover its policy regarding sibling splits, how that policy came into being, and how the system implements the policy. As part of the last question, you will also want to know the official and unofficial policies regarding sibling splits.

One major tenet of the child welfare system calls for placing children in the least restrictive environment possible. That means that children should stay with their parents if possible, but if that is not possible then they should live in an environment closest to their biological setting. Least restrictive placements include relative care, foster home, group home, residential facility, and finally a locked residential facility. When making a placement, adoption workers should always make decisions in the best interest of the child. Most importantly, a least restrictive placement means that siblings stay together.

When a sibling group enters foster care, a significant part of the assessment includes if workers should place them together. The history of child welfare tells us that this was not always the case. There are countless numbers of siblings separated and placed in different homes all over the country, leading to people not knowing they had siblings until later in adulthood. Some people live their lives never knowing they had siblings.

Currently, every state has its own policy regarding adoption and sibling placement. I know of states with different policies regarding sibling splits occurring in different parts of the state. In some local communities, the child welfare agency, judges, and prosecutors make placement decisions without a clear policy regarding the impact the placement might have on the children.

Let me give you an example of two termination cases before two different judges in different counties of the same state. In these two cases, there was enough testimony for the judges to terminate parental rights. The first judge terminated parental rights when there was enough evidence to do so. The second judge, with the same facts, would not terminate parental rights until an agency had arranged an approved adoptive family. In these cases, children's permanency depended on which county they lived in. In addition, neither county discussed the issue of sibling splits.

Questions

1. In the example, two judges took different approaches in deciding to terminate parental rights. After examining both options, which approach do you think is in the children's best interest? Support your position with information from the professional literature.

2. Examine your local community. What is the policy regarding sibling splits? Is the policy local or statewide? Explain.

3. Now that you have examined the official policy, how do local agencies carry out the policy? Is the issue of sibling splits discussed? Is it more likely that siblings will be split, especially if they are older?

Adoption Worker

I function as an adoption worker in a large, local adoption agency that specializes in finding adoptive homes for children classified with special needs. Generally, children have special needs if they are part of the abuse and neglect, child welfare systems. This means that their primary caretaker abused and/or neglected them and because of this treatment, these children end up in the foster care system. After the state terminates parental rights, special needs children become eligible for adoption. My agency finds adoptive homes for these children. In this case, the residential agency contacted the adoption agency and asked if we could find an adoption home for two children under their care. We agreed to work with the children and the agency to find an adoptive home for the siblings.

Background Information

Sarah, age fourteen, and Robert, age twelve, were siblings living in the Downing Residential Facility for girls and boys with behavioral and/or emotional problems. Their problems dictated that their least restrictive placement be a residential home. Sarah and Robert came to the attention of the child welfare division when they were seven and five years old, respectively. The children were living with their parents in a rural community. Their parents, Donald and Judith Beck, had been married for 10 years. During that time, the Becks had a chaotic marriage. Their parents complained about domestic violence, sometimes resulting in windows broken out of the house. At different times, the Becks and their neighbors called the police.

Sarah and Robert came from unstructured family environments. Their parents had moved to the United States from England to work for the government. They were a Caucasian couple in their early thirties. Sarah and Robert were born in the United States and were U.S. citizens. The Becks enjoyed entertaining, going to parties, and other social events. Beginning when they were young, Sarah and Robert's parents often left them home alone. While there was no evidence of physical abuse, there was evidence of neglect. Sarah was responsible for much of Robert's care. When her parents went out at night, Sarah fed and dressed Robert. When Robert started school, Sarah got him up in the morning and made sure he was dressed. Sarah also helped Robert with his homework before starting on her own homework each night. Because of her parents' drinking, they were not always able to tend to the children's needs.

Sarah and Robert witnessed a lot of the yelling and fighting between their parents. Donald and Judith would have massive fights where furnishings were broken. They hit each other, threw things, and destroyed televisions, lamps, plates, and windows. Their fights would go on for hours at a time. During some of the big fights, Sarah would take Robert to her bedroom, and they would hide in the closet until their parents had stopped fighting, and went out, or went to bed. After the fighting stopped, Sarah would put Robert in his room with some toys, and she would clean the house.

A Child's Nightmare

One evening while Sarah and Robert were in the family room playing, they heard their parents yelling at each other. Both children left the family room, walked to the hallway, and stood at the bottom of the stairs. Their parents were at the top of the stairs hitting and screaming at each other. Their mother had a baseball bat in her hands. She swung it at their father but missed. Instead, the bat hit a mirror hanging on the wall and it shattered, falling to the floor, with some of the pieces bouncing down the stairs. Donald was not wearing shoes and he began screaming about cutting his feet on the glass. While he was looking down at the glass, Judith swung the bat a second time hitting Donald in the arm. He fell back against the wall, stepped into more glass, and screamed again from the pain.

Sarah cried out. Judith turned to see where the noise was coming from. When Judith turned, Donald moved quickly and grabbed Judith from behind. They did not see the knife in his hand until it moved across their mother's throat. The blood, shooting out in every direction covered Donald, the wall, and the railing. When Donald let her go, Judith's body tumbled down the stairs and landed at the children's feet.

Sarah and Robert stood, looking down at their dead mother. She was not moving. Her blood ran along the floor toward their feet. They could hear their father at the top of the stairs sobbing. They looked up and saw him on the floor saying, "I'm sorry," repeatedly. Robert reached down to touch his mother. He called her name but there was no reply.

When the police arrived at the house, both children were sitting on the floor beside their mother's body. Robert laid his head on her chest, while Sarah stroked her mother's hair. Neither child was crying, nor did they react to the police coming into the house.

The first police officer asked the children where their father was. Sarah, never making eye contact with the police officer, briefly looked up the stairs and then back down at her mother. A second police officer came into the hallway and said he would stay with the children while the other officer looked for Donald. As the first officer started up the stairs, he heard a single gun shot. As he moved up the stairs, the other police officer picked up Sarah and Robert and moved them out of the house.

Sarah and Robert were placed in the state foster care system. Their mother and father were dead. According to the police report, Donald called the police, waited until they arrived so the children would not be alone, and then shot himself in the head.

Most of the information about that night came from Sarah after years of therapy. Because Robert was younger, his recollection of the events was not as clear. However, for years after that night, both children had nightmares and did not want to sleep in separate rooms.

Questions

It is difficult to imagine a more horrifying event for children than to see their father murder their mother and then commit suicide. Perhaps it was best that Robert was too young to remember. However, Sarah did remember the events and they haunted her for years. Given the unusual nature of this event, please respond to the following questions.

1. Examine the professional literature about childhood trauma. See if the literature discusses this type of event. If not, find other types of trauma that might come closest to this in the lives of children. Based on your examination, describe the different types of childhood trauma and the emotional and behavioral effects it can have on children.

2. From the literature, what are some of the short- and long-term effects of untreated childhood trauma? What presentation would you expect to find from children who had experienced this kind of traumatic event in their lives?

3. If you were the adoption worker for this case, what would your first hunch be about how to proceed with these children? How would you engage these children in therapy?

Foster Care

After Sarah and Robert were placed in foster care, their foster care worker looked for relatives that could care for the children. Since Donald and Judith were from England, they had no relatives in the United States. The worker contacted their relatives in England, but none wanted to provide care for the children. The funeral and interment of Donald and Judith occurred in the United States, and no family or friends from England attended. Sarah and Robert did not attend the funeral because no one knew if they would understand what was happening or how they would emotionally handle the service.

Question

Examine the literature on grief and loss in childhood. Based on your findings and personal experience, was the decision to exclude the children from their parents' funerals appropriate? Provide an argument for and against allowing them to attend the funeral based on the literature and your experience.

The original foster care agency asked the foster parents if they wanted to adopt Sarah and Robert. They declined, saying that they only wished to be their foster parents. The family saw themselves providing a temporary shelter for children in need. Moreover, they thought that Robert's behavior was too disruptive and they did not think they could handle him long term.

State law gives foster parents the opportunity to adopt their foster children if a child remains in a foster home for six months or more. In these instances, the court views foster parents and blood relatives as equals in future decision making. If a foster parent and a relative both want to adopt the same child, the foster care agency conducts a home-study on both families and recommends to the court which family would best meet the needs of the child. The placement objective is always based on the "best interest of the child."

Questions

Regardless of your field of practice, as a practitioner you will face issues pertaining to the foster care system during your practice career. This is especially true if you work with children, adolescents, and families in any practice setting. Therefore, it behooves you to understand the foster care and adoptive system in your locale.

1. Examine the literature and local sources to determine the law in your state regarding the rights of foster parents and relatives when it comes to permanent placement decisions for children.

2. Based on your findings, professional experience, and/or dialogue with classmates, present an argument about why the courts should or should not treat foster parents and relatives equally.

3. What are some reasons why a relative would not want to have the children in their home under foster care, but would want to adopt children when they were free for adoption?

After their placement in foster care, the foster care agency's medical doctor diagnosed Robert with Attention Deficient Hyperactivity Disorder (ADHD). He had a difficult time listening and following instructions. He would fight with his foster parents, including throwing things at them. His schoolwork was poor. He had difficulty sitting in his chair in school. He hit more than one teacher after they asked him to stop being disruptive in class. When he was sent to the principal's office, he could not sit in one place. He would talk to everyone that came into the office.

Through consultation with two doctors, Robert began taking Ritalin. With Ritalin, his behavior improved. However, he began losing weight and falling asleep in class and at home. He completed more homework because he could focus for longer periods. Nevertheless, once Robert was home from school and completed his homework, he was too tired to do anything else. He did not play with the children in the neighborhood, interact with his sister, watch television, or play. All he wanted to do was sleep. The doctor kept adjusting his medication, but they could not find a middle ground dose that controlled his ADHD symptoms and allowed him to be an active child.

Questions

There is much controversy about the overprescribing of Ritalin. There are two basic arguments about the diagnoses of ADHD and Ritalin. The first argument is that because of the controversy, children who should be on Ritalin are not receiving the appropriate treatment. This is a disservice to children, because they are not allowed to reach their full potential. The second argument is that too many children are being diagnosed as ADHD and placed on Ritalin because the parents and teachers want a quick fix instead of spending the time necessary to address the behavior. These people believe that Ritalin is prescribed more for the comfort of adults that to meet the needs of children.

1. Examine the professional literature on this subject. What are the statistics on the use of Ritalin in your state? How does your state compare nationally and to the national average?

2. According to the literature, how does the drug work, and what are the effects and side effects of Ritalin on children? What does the literature say happens to children taking Ritalin or other drugs for ADHD that are misdiagnosed?

Sarah was also having problems after her mother and father's murder-suicide. Sarah was diagnosed with Selective Mutism. After her mother died, Sarah stopped interacting with people. She would say few words and kept mostly to herself. She did not play with the children in the neighborhood or at the school. In the foster home, she stayed in her room. Sarah would do her homework, sit at the table to eat with the family, and would go everywhere the family took her. Sarah followed all the rules around the house. If told to do something, she would quickly complete the task. Whatever food was put on her plate, she ate it. The foster care worker noted that there were times when the foster mother could tell that Sarah did not like something on her plate. However, Sarah would eat her food without saying a word.

Second Foster Home

Sarah and Robert stayed in their first foster home for eleven months. The foster mother found Robert's behavior too disruptive and she felt sorry that she could not handle his behavior. Robert would fight with the foster parents. He broke things, stole money and jewelry, and hurt a couple of the neighbor's pets.

The family was willing to keep Sarah, but the foster care worker did not want to separate the children. She noted that because of the trauma they had experienced, their only support was from each other. If they were split, it would only further lead to their feeling of abandonment. The foster care worker understood that she was denying permanency for Sarah, but she thought that she could find a home for both children. Therefore, the worker had to find another foster home for the siblings.

Sarah and Robert remained in their first foster home until the worker found a second foster home. According to the reports, the children met with the foster parents two times before they were placed. Their second foster home was a two-parent family in their early fifties. Their biological children were in the home and they had been foster parents for over twenty years.

While in foster care, the agency also searched for an adoptive family for the children. However, because of their behaviors, the foster care agency decided that the children were not ready for an adoptive placement. They wanted the children to receive more therapy before they placed them for adoption.

They lived in the second foster home for fourteen months. During that time, Robert was diagnosed with Conduct Disorder and Oppositional Defiant Disorder. In the second foster home, his behavior became worse. Robert fought with the older biological children in the family. He also stole and destroyed their belongings. If one of the older children had something Robert wanted, he would try to take it. When he was stopped, Robert would wait and take the item when no one was around and destroy it. He stole toys, games, and clothing from everyone in the house. When Robert was mad at one of the teenagers, he found ways to get back at them. On more than one occasion, he got up in the middle of the night, took their homework or project, and destroyed it. The next morning, the biological teenager wanted to "kill" Robert. The foster parents struggled with how to provide a safe environment for Robert and maintain peace in the household. However, he never stole anything from his sister. They did not interact with each other in the foster home, and he never touched any of her things.

Sarah, who was still a Selective Mute, was also diagnosed with Separation Anxiety Disorder. The foster care worker thought that all of her loses took a toll on her physically and emotionally. Her schoolwork declined and she did not interact with anyone in the foster home.

A Third Placement: Group Home

At the ages of nine and seven, the foster care agency decided to place Sarah and Robert in a group home. They thought that both children needed intensive counseling and that a group home was the most appropriate setting. In assessing their behavior, the foster care worker thought a traditional foster home placement no longer met their needs. The foster care agency made the referral to the group home for placement.

The group home offered two types of treatment. First, they each received individual counseling twice a week. Second, they received group counseling two days a week. The groups were divided by gender. The group home hoped that the intense counseling would address their behavioral and emotional issues.

The children lived in the group home for three years. They participated in individual and groups counseling, went to school, and were exposed to cultural and entertainment events. Sarah and Robert had settled into group home living and there was no further discussion about finding an adoptive home. In the second year, Sarah began to speak. In her individual therapy sessions, Sarah drew pictures, painted, and played with toys. She mostly painted houses, farms, parks, and people playing. Her drawings demonstrated no clear signs about the abuse and neglect she suffered.

During one session, Sarah drew a picture of people playing in a park. She went through the crayons, adding bright colors to her picture. Picking through the box she appeared to be looking for something. The therapist said nothing, but watched her closely. When Sarah could not find what she was looking for, she turned to the therapist and said, "Do you have yellow?" The therapist was surprised, but tried not to show it on her face. She looked around, found a yellow crayon, and gave it to Sarah. She colored in a yellow sun and then showed the picture to the therapist. From that point on, she talked to the therapist, but nobody else.

Sarah did not interact with the other children, but she would talk in the individual sessions. If they were working on a project, Sarah would ask for help. She also began asking for help with her homework. Her conversations dealt with school, games she played in the individual sessions, or books she read. She did not talk about her parents or her life before foster care, which included her brother. From the time that Sarah became a selective mute, she never interacted with her brother.

During his time in the group home, Robert's behavior improved. The number of fights and stealing decreased. The therapist believed that they had controlled his medication, and that it had a positive affect on his behavior. In school, he sat through most of each class. In the individual counseling sessions, he talked about feeling as if he could not control himself. He described times when he felt like he was watching himself steal something or get into a fight. He was telling himself to stop, but he could not. He said he wanted to be alone with the other children at the group home, but he did not think he would be able to control himself.

Robert had difficulty in therapy groups. He found it hard to sit still while the other children talked. He talked out of turn, got out of his seat, or picked on other children until the group leader sent him out of the room. However, the group therapist noted in the case records that Robert showed improvement in his behavior. All of the negative behaviors had decreased and Robert could participate in parts of every session.

Adoption: Together or Split?

With the improvements of both children in the group home, the conversation turned once again to adoption. The therapist and the group home workers wondered if the children could be adopted. There was some disagreement about their readiness. Sarah's therapist thought that she was ready for an adoptive family. She thought that with no other children in the home, Sarah would bond to the adoptive family. If there were other children, she thought that Sarah would retreat into herself and stop talking. The therapist thought that Sarah would not benefit from competition between her and other children in the home.

They wondered if Sarah and her brother should be placed together. Sarah's therapist said no. She thought that Robert's problems would lessen Sarah's chances of finding a home, and his behavior could result in the adoptive placement disrupting. The adoptive family would have to focus so much time on Robert's behavior, that Sarah would be lost in her own house. She thought Sarah would lose in the competition for parental attention with her brother every time.

The therapist who ran groups for both Sarah and Robert felt the children should stay together. She looked at their history and thought that they had a bond that would hurt them both if they were not in physical contact with each other. Although there was no interaction, they both knew where each other was and that each was safe. She pointed to the fact that while in their foster homes and the group home, Robert never did anything to harm or harass his sister.

While in the group home, four adoption agencies contacted the foster care worker with an adoptive family for Sarah. They tried to find a home for both children, but were unsuccessful. One adoption agency had a home for both children, but they had teenage boys in the home and the adoptive family did not want to put a girl in that environment.

In reviewing the foster care, group home, and residential records, the foster care agency, the group home, the state child welfare department, and the judge met about this case. They discussed the length of time Sarah and Robert had been in care, their treatment progress, and why they had not been adopted. Their history and treatment progress were outlined in the meeting. The group home and the foster care agency both thought that progress was slow, but that the children were improving. The judge asked if treatment that was more intensive would speed their progress.

She also wanted to know if the children should be split in order for them to be adopted. The final decision was to keep the children together.

A Fourth Placement: Residential Treatment

The team decided to place both children in a residential facility. They thought a more intensive environment would address their issues and make it easier to find an adoptive home. Most of the professionals involved in the case wanted the children adopted together, and agreed that the children needed more treatment. The state child welfare department looked for the first residential facility that could provide the treatment and take both children. Three months later, Sarah and Robert were placed in the Downing Residential Facility.

The Downing facility was located about four hours from the group home. For all of their lives, Sarah and Robert have lived in the same city. Their biological home, foster homes, and group home were all within 15 minutes of each other. Now they were moving to an unfamiliar area, to a strange school and had no connections with the families they lived with or the staff they had come to depend on.

Sarah and Robert were placed in the Downing facility because of their intensive counseling and group work. In the facility, Sarah and Robert received two days of individual counseling and five days of group counseling each week. In addition, for the first time, Sarah and Robert received thirty minutes of joint family counseling three times a week. It was determined by the group counselor that if they were to be placed together, it was important for them to interact with each other.

For the first three months, Sarah and Robert continued to function as they did in all their other settings. That is, they did not interact with each other. In the family sessions, Robert would talk about what had happened since the last session while Sarah talked very little. She talked in the individual sessions and talked a little in the group sessions after the first two months, but she only talked about how she was feeling that day in the family session. Sarah never talked about or to Robert.

Questions

Now that the author has presented more information about Sarah and Robert, and before reading further, perform the following exercises based on your education, experience, the professional literature, and the available best practice evidence. To increase your learning potential, you may want to do this in a small group with other students in your course.

1. Based on the information contained above, construct a three-generation genogram and eco-map that represents Sarah and Robert's personal, familial, and environmental circumstances. What further information do you need to complete this exercise? What patterns do these two important graphical assessment tools demonstrate?

2. Develop a list of Sarah and Robert's issues and strengths, drawing from multi-systemic sources.

3. Write a two- to three-page narrative assessment that encompasses Sarah and Robert's multi-systemic issues and strengths. Review Chapter 1 if needed. This narrative should provide a comprehensive and multi-systemic explanation of their life. Below we offer a few questions to guide this process:

- **What are your hunches regarding Sarah and Robert's view of themselves as developing people and as siblings?**
- **What are your hunches about their feelings regarding adolescent identity and their life experiences?**
- **What are your hunches regarding their ability to settle together in a family environment?**
- **What are your hunches about the role and function of their symptoms, including Sarah's selective mutism and Robert's aggressive behavior?**
- **Try to identify the theoretical model or approach that you use to guide your assessment. According to the literature, what other theoretical options are available and how would these change the nature of your assessment?**

4. Develop multi-axial DSM-IV-TR diagnoses for Sarah and Robert. Provide a list of client symptoms that you used to justify your diagnostic decision. What, if any, information was missing that would make this an easier task?

5. Based on what you have read, would you place Sarah and Robert together in a residential facility or split them up and place them in different adoptive homes? Support your position.

6. Sarah and Robert moved from a less restrictive setting to a more restrictive setting. If child welfare always wants to place children in the least restrictive environment, why do you think they made the decision to go in the other direction? What is your position about this decision? Support your position.

The Referral

Sarah and Robert had lived in the Downing facility for sixteen months when they contacted my adoption agency to find an adoptive placement. We had placed children from the Downing Facility in the past, and they asked if we would recruit an adoption home for Sarah and Robert.

My first job after being assigned the case was to gather as much information about Sarah and Robert as I could. I had to write a child assessment on each as part of the written documents on the case. A child assessment is a detailed biological, physical, psychological, emotional, environment, and cultural assessment of the person you are working with. It is comprehensive in its detail and description. The child assessment also helped the potential adoptive family by providing them with as much information as possible about the children they were considering for adoption.

Special needs adoption is a specialized field of practice. When discussing adoption, people's culture, history, and life experiences all play a part in what they think about adoption. I have worked with families where their extended family refused to recognize the adoptive children in the family. There were grandparents who only bought Christmas presents for the biological children and not the adoptive children. Relatives would ask not to have the adoptive children in family pictures. Family and friends often disappear instead of support new adoptive parents. When working in adoption, it is important to understand the history, practices, and issues that can affect families wanting to adopt.

History of Adoption Laws

Historically, adoption has been addressed in many cultures. From the time Moses turned on his adopted family to lead his biological family out of bondage, to a blended family when Joseph married Jesus' mother (this could also have been the first written evidence of an open adoption, because Jesus knew who his father was and had regular contact with him), to an infertile couple who adopted a baby and called him Clark Kent, adoption has been a part of recorded, unrecorded, and fictional history since the beginning of people on this planet (Pertman, 2000).

One of the earlier recordings of adoption,

> . . . appears in the Code of Hammurabi, drafted by the Babylonians around 2285 B.C., which provided that if a man has taken a young child from the waters to sonship and has reared him up no one has any claim against the nursing. (Carp, 1998, p. 3)

Adoptions have been found in Egypt, China, Rome, Greece, other Asian countries, Africa, and throughout ancient and tribal societies (Carp, 1998; Pertman, 2000). Some cultures adopted in order to have a male heir. Other cultures adopted the families of the men who were lost in war:

> It is believed, for example, that in Rome, China and other ancient civilizations, many infertile couples and parents who had only daughters formally adopted adult males to serve as heirs, to carry on family names or to participate in religious ceremonies. (Pertman, 2000, p. 15)

Terrell and Modell (1994) found that in many Pacific Island Tahitian and Trukese societies, adoption was a natural part of their cultural existence. In those cultures, the term *kinship* extended to the entire community. Their practices included someone in the community parenting a child when the biological parents were unable to provide care. It ensured that families that could meet their needs cared for all children. Often these practices included the biological family maintaining a relationship with the child throughout his life. Through adoption, the child's support system increased because there were more kin to meet the child's needs.

In Western society, 16th century England is an excellent example about how adoptions were perceived and controlled. In English common law, there was no mention of adoption. The power of the church and the law were the major deterrents to adoption. The church placed emphasis on blood relations. Adoptions were discouraged because of their impact on inheritance. The church, in denouncing adoption, implied that adopted children were born from incest. There was much public scrutiny, and in some European cultures, adoption was seen as unchristian (Carp, 1998).

English common law did not recognize adoption. The laws were written to protect the property rights of blood relationships (Carp, 1998).

> English common law, on which America's founders modeled our own legal system, did not refer to adoption at all; in fact, it wasn't until 1926 that England approved its first generalized adoption statute. Scholars believe the nation saw no need for organized adoption because inheritance was dependent solely on bloodlines and children without relatives to care for them were placed in almshouse, then made apprentices or indentured servants at very young ages. (Pertman, 2000, p. 15)

The colonies that became the United States carried on the traditions of the English Poor Laws and Charitable Choice. They upheld the belief that blood relationships were most important and should be held above all others. However, there were differences in need in the United States than in England. The need for farm labor in the 1700s produced "informal transfers," the placing of large numbers of children to work on plantations. The Industrial Revolution produced so many homeless children that a demand grew to provide services for them. Charitable organizations began the mission of finding permanent homes for children (Pertman, 2000).

Throughout history, societies have found ways to care for children whose biological parents were unable to provide for them. In the United States, "in the 17th and 18th centuries children were placed in foundling homes provided by the state" (Rosenberg, 1992, p. 9). If the child survived infancy in the foundling houses, they were placed in the labor force, or put on orphan trains and adopted by farm families who made them field hands (Rosenberg, 1992).

In 1851, Massachusetts established the first adoption statute that included control of adoption (Rosenberg, 1992; Pertman, 2000). Up until that point children were placed in almshouses or some type of residential facility. Charitable and religious organizations began to arrange adoptions for those children (Rosenberg, 1992).

According to Rosenberg (1992), "In 1912 the United States Children's Bureau was established as the first public child welfare agency" (p. 9). Prior to the Children's Bureau, adoption was not addressed in the country in any tangible way. Around 1912 charitable organizations, lawyers, and agencies began to place children for adoption (Rosenberg, 1992). By 1929, every state had some kind of adoption law. It was also during this time that the Children's Aid Society, followed by other organizations, began relocating children to the south on "orphan trains" (Pertman, 2000).

In 1974, the passage of the Child Abuse Prevention and Treatment Act (PL 93-247) increased the number of children entering the foster care system (McRoy, 1999). The child abuse act was the federalizing of Children's Protective Services (CPS), in that every state had to pass and implement CPS laws, policies, and investigation systems to protect children. The Adoption Opportunity Act of 1978 and the 1980 Adoption Assistance and Child Welfare Act included provisions to find adoptive homes, provide adoption subsidies, and to develop post-adoption services (McRoy, 1999).

The 1980 PL 96-272 Adoptions and Opportunities Act placed an emphasis on permanency for children and provided money to states for making adoption placements. Other important policies and laws included the Adoption 2002 initiative calling for a doubling of the number of foster care adoptions, the 1994 Multiethnic Placement Act, the amended 1996 Interethnic Adoption Provisions, and the 1997 Adoption and Safe Family Act (Bartholet, 1999; National Adoption Information Clearinghouse, 2002). All the changes have placed more focus on permanency for children.

Decrease in Infant Adoptions

In the United States, as in other countries, there is a cultural belief in reproduction. People grow up thinking about having children, not adopting children.

> Ours is a society that glorifies reproduction, drives the infertile to pursue treatment at all costs, socializes them to think of adoption as a second-class form of parenting to be pursued only as a last resort, and regulates adoption in a way that makes it difficult, degrading, and expensive. (Bartholet, 1999, p. 181)

The number of infants available for adoption has decreased. "The social and sexual revolution of the 1960s, the development of more effective birth control measures, and the legitimization of abortion in the 1970s all had a profound effect on adoption practices" (Rosenberg, 1992, p. 10).

From 1952 to 1988, the percent of premarital births placed for adoption declined from 8.7% to 2% (National Adoption Information Clearinghouse, 2002). A study by Bachrach, London, and Maza, stated that the decline in infants being placed for adoption was primarily due to the declining number of white women placing their children for adoption (1991).

All of the above factors have reduced the availability of infants for adoption. Therefore, many of those people who wanted to adopt an infant turn to adopting special needs children.

Defining Special Needs

There is no agreement about what constitutes special needs adoption. There are public, private, and independent agencies placing children for adoption and each has their own definition of what are special needs. Children who would be classified as special needs in one state may not have that designation in another state (Watson, 1996).

Pertman provided an overview of the range of children who could be defined as special needs.

> But more than 117,000 of them—teenagers who have bounced into and out of innumerable foster homes, infants with emotional or physical disabilities, babies born to prostitutes and people with HIV, and children of all ages who are black, Hispanic or mixed race, or possess other special needs are available for adoption. (Pertman, 2000, p. 157)

In some states, minority children are classified as special needs by virtue of their race. Minority children carried the label of special needs because agencies thought they were hard to place (Howe, 1998; Pertman, 2000).

Intact Adoptions

Most adoptions do not disrupt. Over 80% of adoptions remained intact (Groze & Rosenberg, 1998). In fact, adoption disruptions (before finalization) and adoption dissolutions (after finalization) were low, compared to the number of adoptions that remained intact. Groze (1996) found that 78% of parents were positive about the adoption and by the fourth year, 69% of parents were happy. There is consensus that the majority of adoptions remained intact.

McRoy (1999, pp. 70–71) identified and listed factors for agencies and adoptive parents that served to stabilize the adoption.

Agency and Worker Factors

- Communication with adoptive family
- Good match
- Awareness of child's needs

Adoptive Parents Factors

- Strong commitment
- Strong marriage
- Communication with child
- Openness to seek professional help
- Previous parenting experience

- Previous parenting experience with special needs children
- Support system
- Outside community involvement
- Realistic expectations and flexibility
- Positive personality characteristics
- Maturity/stability

Numerous systems played an important role in maintaining adoptions. One often overlooked area was that intact adoptions included the involvement of the biological children in the adoption journey. Biological children of adoptive parents who were more involved in the adoption discussions and had a better understanding of adoption resulted in fewer adoption disruptions. Mullin and Johnson (1999) found that it was important for the adoption worker to spend time with the biological children in their home.

The involvement of the biological children in the adoption allowed the adoption worker to gain a greater understanding of the children's needs, what they know about adoption, and ways to help the adoptive parents to resolve those concerns with their children (Mullin & Johnson, 1999). The adoption worker must be an advocate for the biological children, educator for the parents, and have the skills to connect families to resources when appropriate (Mullin & Johnson, 1999).

Adoptive families were more successful when there was "the mutual support of family members, including fathers who were prepared to become actively involved in child care as well as supported mothers, helped both children and adults gain emotional strength" (Howe, 1998, p. 105). One study by Barth and Berry (1988) showed that there were fewer disruptions when relatives lived within visiting distances.

Adoption Disruptions/Dissolutions

One of the most important outcomes regarding adoption had to do with children achieving permanency in the adoptive home. When children are placed in an adoptive home, the hope is that they stay there until they reach the age of maturity, and move out as a part of the natural transition to adulthood. However, some children do not achieve permanency. For them, a disruption or dissolution becomes their destiny. The literature defines the two concepts as follows:

> The term *disruption* is used to describe an adoption which does not continue, resulting in the child returning to foster care and/or to another set of adoptive parent(s). The term *dissolution* is used to describe an adoption that fails after finalization, resulting in the child returning to foster care and/or another set of adoptive parent(s). (National Adoptive Information Clearinghouse, 2002)

A review of the literature found little distinction between disruptions and dissolutions. If an adoption ended anytime during the placement and supervision, it was called a disruption (Howe, 1998). Supervision of the adoption placement meant that the adoption agency maintained contact with the adoptive family for generally between 6 months to 1 year after the adoptive child was placed in the home. This supervision continued until a judge finalized the adoption.

However, the literature discussed a number of indicators that could lead to disruptions. One major theme from the adoptive parents' perspective was the lack of preparation about special needs adoption and the lack of information about the child they were adopting. Barth and Berry (1988) completed a study where 20% of adoptive parent(s) said the agency did nothing to help them learn about adoption and 60% of parent(s) said the agency did not prepare them for the adoption. Berry (1990) found "that satisfaction with agency preparation was the second most critical predictor of the parents' satisfaction with the entire adoption, second only to the child's ability to attach" (p. 407). In that same study, 53% of the parent(s) said the agency told them about the child, while 73% of adoption workers said that they had informed the family about the child. Berry found that the parent(s) and the workers had different perceptions of the behavioral needs of the child. Rosenthal and Groze (1990) found that 35% of adoptive parent(s) said they received insufficient information and 44% of parent(s) said the adoption worker was not helpful or only somewhat helpful.

A number of studies identified what they called common problems faced by adoptive parents. Bean (1984), Hartman (1984), Kadushin and Martin (1988), and Barth and Berry (1988) all wrote about these common problems as not only affecting the daily functioning of the family, but playing an important role in determining if the placement could be maintained or end in a disruption. These common problems were broken down into six areas:

1. Biological parents may want to maintain contact with their children. This could be a threat to the adoptive parent(s), who are trying to develop their own parenting authority. In addition, unlike infant adoption, most special needs children will know their birth parent(s), and depending on their age, know how to get in touch with them.
2. How to help the child with issues of entitlement. This addresses the issue of how a child becomes a member of the family. If families have responsibilities divided up, what is taken away from existing members of the family to be given to the new member, and how will people respond to the change?
3. Struggling with how to help the child fit into the home without changing all the rules. This would include things such as what time people go to bed, family activities, beliefs, types of food, and recreational activities.
4. Developing rituals that will include the adoptive child.
5. How parent(s) can meet their own needs while meeting the child's needs.
6. Reactions of family, friends, and community to adopting a child.

In a publication by the U.S. Department of Health and Human Services (2002), three kinds of problems were cited as leading to an adoption disruption:

(1) unrecognized pre-existing problems, (2) pre-existing problems that are known but left unexplored, and (3) unpredictable problems that occur after placement.

The age of the children has a significant impact on the stability of the adoption, ". . . with older children who have behavioral and emotional problems experiencing higher rates of disruption" (Groze & Rosenberg, 1998, p. 1). "Adoption studies regularly confirm that age at the time of placement is the key predictor for how well adopted children will do" (Bartholet, 1999, p.179). The older the child, the more likely the adoption could disrupt.

Adopted children were overrepresented in mental health services (Groze & Rosenberg, 1998). It is possible that the number of children and families needing mental health services was higher than those actually receiving services. Families may not have recognized the need for services. Others may have believed that they would be viewed as bad parents if they sought help.

Several studies compared adopted and non-adopted children on issues of behavior, relationships, and academic work (Brodzinsky, Lang, & Smith, 1995; Stein & Hoopes, 1985; Wierzbicki, 1993). A review of the research revealed that adopted children had more emotional, academic, and behavioral problems than did non-adopted children. However, Priel, Melamed-Hass, Besser, and Kantor (2000) found no significant differences between the two groups. There appears to be some debate regarding which variables to look at when comparing the two groups.

Another area of discussion concerned adopted children maintaining contact with biological family, fictive kin, and friends in their life after the adoption. That concept was referred to as an open adoption. The debate was over the impact of open and closed adoption on children. Some professionals took the position that children in closed adoptions experienced identity problems because of the lack of contact with their biological family (Frasch, Brooks, & Barth, 2000). Grotevant, McRoy, Elde, and Fravel (1994) recommended that a level of openness should be developed between adoptive parents and biological parents.

Another area that the literature explored regarding disruptions concerned adoptive families with less success when they had a difficult time maintaining an open, supportive, unconditional relationship with children (Howe, 1998). A family, which could be viewed as a closed system, may have produced an environment that was difficult for the adoptive child to function in appropriately.

Another area of adoption that has not received much attention is the community into which the child was adopted (Miall, 1996). If the community was not supportive of special needs adoption, it may have placed more stress on the family.

The data showed that the higher the family's socioeconomic status, the greater the possibility of the adoption being disrupted (Groze & Rosenberg, 1998). Parents with higher socioeconomic status may have placed unreasonable expectations of achievement and behavior on the adoptive child that the child may not be able to meet.

Finally, Howe (1998) found that 70–80% of adoptive parents reported satisfaction with their adoption. He also found that disruptions increased with the age of the child. There was a 10% disruption rate for children under 10 and a 20–40% disruption rate for children over age 10. "Adoption studies regularly confirm that age at the time of placement is the key predictor for how well adopted children will do" (Bartholet, 1999, p. 179).

Adoptive Families

Some studies looked at disruption based on demographic information. Rosenthal and Groze (1990) and Berry (1990) found fewer disruptions with families traditionally screened out of the adoption process. Families who were screened out may not have met the state guidelines for being adoptive parents, or they may not have met the values of the agency doing the determination. Single parents, low-income families, minority families, and families with other children in the home were less likely to experience a disruption (Rosenthal & Groze, 1990).

Single, low-income, and minority parents appeared to have more reasonable expectations for their adoptive children. Middle- and upper-income families, those with mothers who had a college education, and families with no other children in the home were more likely to experience a disruption.

Researchers found that middle income parents appeared to have higher and sometimes unrealistic expectations for their adoptive children. Because the children could not live up to the parents' expectations, it increased the conflict in the home and resulted in a disruption. Some research showed that families with more education have more problems when adopting older children. Parents with a high school education had more success with older adoptions than parents with college degrees (Howe, 1998). The parents were more accepting of the child and the behavior and, therefore, the child was not viewed as a disappointment.

Barth and Berry (1988) identified other barriers to a successful adoptive placement. A lack of social support, the transition from not having a child to having a child, establishing a parenting role with the child, managing the child's behavior, and the parents coping response all affected the success of the placement.

There was little research on the role of biological children in the maintaining or disrupting of an adoption. Mullin and Johnson found that agencies needed to prepare biological children for the adoptive children who were going to become part of the family: "The adoption of a child with special needs may be more likely to disrupt when the parents believe that the toll the placement is taking on their birth/previously adopted children is more than they can manage" (1999, p. 2). The biological children may not have participated in the adoption discussion.

Mullin and Johnson (1999), in reviewing adoption literature, found that having biological and adopted children in the same home increased the chance of a disruption. The introduction of a new child to the family disrupted the equilibrium of the family. The adoptive child interrupted the relationships, roles, and rules in the family. They also found that the emotional atmosphere in the home changed. Parents spent more time with the adopted children, while other family members received less attention, and the parents became drained with all the new needs and responsibilities (Mullin & Johnson, 1999).

Family Formation

Kirk (1964) and Brodzinsky (1990) discussed three models of self-perception among adoptive families. First, there were families that rejected/denied the differences and created a less open and less reality-based environment. Second, there were the families that focused on differences and ascribed blame for difficulties to genetics or pre-adoptive history. Third, there were families that acknowledge the difference openly, sharing concerns and feelings about their adoptive status.

Adoptive Children

Adopted children may have experienced a number of placements before they were adopted. First, they were removed from the birth family. Children may have developed self-narratives that explained that they were the reason why they were removed from their birth homes (Groze & Rosenberg, 1998). If the child was removed from the foster home, that may have reinforced his or her belief that he or she was the cause of the problems in the home.

Harm to Children

There was general agreement in the literature that adoption disruptions were harmful to the child and the family. Children who experienced a disruption were less likely to be adopted in the future. Those children tended to have more behavioral problems, showed a lack of respect for authority, felt they needed to protect themselves, and were more likely to have had some mental health label (Kadushin & Martin, 1988).

It was also important to remember the circumstances that brought the child into the adoptive system. Watson wrote:

> Most special-needs children enter adoption because they were living in a family that could not meet their needs. Some are born the victims of prenatal substance abuse. Many experienced traumatic abuse in their families of origin or in foster families. Statistics indicate that 75% of the children currently in foster care have experienced some sexual abuse, as have 85% of children placed in adoption since 1983. (1996, p. 532)

Each time a child was moved to a new environment, the child was expected to adapt to the new setting. Although there were changes in each setting (rules, relationships, food, expectations, history), the child was expected to adjust to that environment (Hartman, 1984). The child had no history with the family. The family's lifestyle, beliefs, secrets, and interactions were all foreign to the child. However, the child was expected to conform to each environment.

All families have a life story that travels with them throughout the generations. That life story included values, beliefs, history, stories and, for some, a family bond. The literature terms that a narrative (Groze & Rosenberg, 1998). Adopted children experienced a broken narrative when moved from their biological home and placed in foster care.

Further moves broke the narrative for every foster home the child was placed in, until the child was finally placed in an adoptive home. In the adoptive home, the child came into an environment that was intergenerational. The history, values, and culture of the family were passed down from one generation to the next. However, the adoptive child does not know the history, rules, secrets, or relationships of the adoptive family. It takes time for him to learn and understand that history (Groze & Rosenberg, 1998). That could prevent the adoptive child from ever being fully a part of the family.

Howe (1998) discussed two theories regarding the development of adoptive children. "The first argues that poor quality care in an emotionally adverse environment during the first year or so of life has long-lasting negative effects on development and personality" (Howe, 1998, p. 72). "The second argues that full developmental recovery is possible if the disturbed child is introduced into a fresh, good quality social environment" (p. 72).

There was some discussion about the psychosocial development of older children placed for adoption. A relationship exists between when the child was placed and his psychosocial adjustment. Children placed in institutional care had the hardest time adjusting. Children placed in foster care and then adopted did better than those in institutional care did, but children not involved in the foster care system had the best psychosocial development (Howe, 1998). This is because of the behaviors often exhibited by adoptive children. "Adopted children in general and late-adopted children in particular appear to show more antisocial, externalizing, acting-out, conduct disordered behavior than non-adopted control populations (Howe, 1998, p. 82).

When looking at special needs children, the issue of personality received major attention.

The following behaviors and personality traits are those most frequently used to describe and identify tendencies in late-adopted children:

- Insecure and anxious
- Attention-seeking and demanding
- Restless
- Poor concentration
- Unpopular with peers and relationship problems with peers
- Lying
- Hostility, anger, and aggression
- Oppositional behavior
- Conduct disorders including criminal behavior
- Improved social adjustment in early adulthood. (Howe, 1998, pp. 87–88)

It is possible to identify three interesting developmental divisions within the broad category of late-placed adoptions. These are based on the character and quality of the children's pre-placement experience. At least three types of early life experience can be discerned in adoption research:

1. Institutional care: No experiences of close, regular intimate relationships and, therefore, no experience of sustained and personalized rejection, abuse, or neglect in relationships with a primary caretaker.
2. Good quality care with main caretaker during the first year or two of life before the relationship takes a turn for the worse and the child experiences loss, abandonment, rejection, abuse and/or neglect in the subsequent years before being placed for adoption.
3. Continuously poor quality care and loss, rejection, abuse and/or neglect during the years prior to being placed for adoption. (Howe, 1998, p. 88)

The literature discussed the impact of the child's behavior on placements. "Prior to the final removal from the birth family, children in disrupted/dissolved adoptions were more likely to have been exhibiting aggressive, acting-out behaviors" (McRoy, 1999, p. 63). Therefore, it was important to look at the child's behavior prior to placement and then to assess how the behaviors manifested themselves in placement. "During the adoptive placement, adopted children in intact placements had significantly decreased their acting-out behaviors, while children in placements that eventually disrupted or dissolved had escalated these behaviors" (McRoy, 1999, p. 65).

Questions

1. The history and definitions provided above are brief. Therefore, examine the professional literature further pertaining to adoption and adoption disruption. Based on your findings, define adoption disruption and dissolution.

2. With the review of some of the issues affecting adoptive children and families, discuss how that information could affect your decision to place Sarah and Robert together or to place them in different homes.

3. Discuss which personality traits of late-adopted children are found in Sarah and Robert.

4. The discussion on adoption disruptions has a direct impact on finding an adoptive home for both children. If Sarah was placed in an adoptive home, and the adoption disrupted, how do you think it would affect her?

The Referral (Continues)

With the additional information on special needs adoption, now we can return to the case of Sarah and Robert. Remember that all of the information you have reviewed will have an effect on your final placement decision.

Sarah and Robert made progress in the Downing facility. Robert's diagnoses of ADHD and oppositional defiant disorder continued at a lesser degree and he no longer showed signs of conduct disorder. Because of that review, his medication was reduced. Sarah's only diagnosis was separation anxiety disorder as she continued to make progress in her therapy sessions.

At the time of my first meeting with them, Sarah was attending public school, had made a number of friends, and was thinking about participating in some school activities. She worked well with the staff and the therapists at the facility. All their reports focused on her growth. She asked for jobs around the facility so she could earn some money. She became a leader, mentored in the group sessions, and talked to the new girls who came to the facility. Sarah asked her counselor if she was well enough to be adopted. She said she wanted to be part of a family. Sarah had seen that some of the other children are adopted from the facility.

Robert was attending the public schools, but all of his classes were special education. He had made progress in a number of areas. Robert could complete some of the tasks in each class, he took his medication each day without fighting with staff, and he participated in the group and individual counseling. Robert would still get into fights with teachers and peers, but there had been a marked decrease in the number of incidents.

The first time I met Sarah and Robert, one of the residential workers participated in the meeting. I introduced myself and talked a little about the adoption agency and my job. I also interacted with the staff person as a way to show Sarah and Robert that I was a safe person to talk with.

I next asked them what they wanted from me. They were quiet for two or three minutes before Sarah broke the silence.

"Can you find us an adoptive family?"

I told them that I would try to find them an adoptive family. I tried to make it clear that my job was to find the best family for them. There may be times when I talked with them about a potential family. However, I might decide that the family was incapable of providing the kind of home I thought was appropriate. I believed it was important for children to understand that the family was not rejecting them, but that I was rejecting the family. They had experienced a lot of rejection in their lives. I wanted to give them some support and show them that they had value and worth. In addition, if I was the one rejecting the families, then any transference would be placed on me and not the families.

While I was recruiting a family for Sarah and Robert, I met with them every two weeks. I wanted to get to know them and I wanted to keep them updated on what was happening. As part of the recruitment, I took a number of steps. By reading all the reports, talking to the professionals involved with the children, and meeting with the children, I was able to put together a detailed child assessment.

Recruiting Families

When recruiting for adoptive families, one of my goals is to make it possible for the family to say that they do not want to adopt a child before ever meeting the child.

To accomplish this goal, I provide the family with as much information as possible. I make a videotape of every child. The tape includes the child answering questions about themselves, what they want the family to know about them, things they enjoy doing, and what they would like in an adoptive family.

To conduct an assessment, my first meeting with a family can be in their home or at the office. When I am ready to make a match, I have the family come to the office. I place them in a conference with the child assessment, the case file, a pad of paper, and a pen. I want them to go through all the information and write down any questions they have. When I come back, we sit down and talk about the information. I answer all of their questions. I also ask them questions about what they read to make sure they did not miss anything. After the meeting, I wait a few days before my next contact with the family to see if they thought of any new questions. We talk about how they are feeling about the process and if they think that they could handle some of the behaviors. We also talk about how they would address those behaviors. I talk with them about the effect of adoption on their family and what kinds of support systems they have, and might need.

If the family wants to continue with the process, the next step is for them to talk to all of the professionals that have been involved in the case. This information will help the family understand how the child interacts on a daily basis. If the family wants to continue with the adoption, I show them the videotape.

The Adoptive Family

I thought one of the families that contacted our agency about adoption was a possible fit for Sarah and Robert. The Welshs, Elliott and Marlene, had contacted the agency about adopting. They were a Caucasian married couple in their mid-forties. Mr. Welsh, age 42, was a manager for a construction company and Mrs. Welsh, age 41, was a vice-president at a manufacturing business. They wanted children, but were unable to have biological children. Mr. Welsh stated that he was sterile, the reason they could not have children. They had known since their early twenties that they were not going to have biological children, so they decided to work on their careers, travel, and participate in a number of charities. In their early forties, they planned to seek an adoption alternative.

Mr. and Mrs. Welsh met at the church they attended. When they were both placed on the same church committee and starting working together, Mr. Welsh asked her out on their first date. During that time, Mrs. Welsh left the state to attend college and Mr. Welsh got a job at a local construction company. After college, Mrs. Welsh returned to her hometown and she and Mr. Welsh began dating again. One year later, they were married.

Mr. Welsh continued to work at the construction company and moved up to manager. Mrs. Welsh worked for several companies until five years earlier when she was hired as a vice-president at her current job. They were active with their families, in their church, and in their community. They volunteered for a number of groups and enjoyed giving their time and money. They also enjoyed planning a trip and traveling each year.

The Welshs reviewed all the information, talked with all the professionals involved with the case, and watched Sarah and Robert's videotape. They thought that they could parent one of the children but were not sure about both of them.

The Placement Decision

Now that you have reviewed the entire case, as the adoption worker, you have to make a decision that will affect Sarah and Robert for the rest of their lives. Where they live, what kind of family they will live in, what type of relationship they will have with each other hinges on your decision.

You could talk the Welshs into adopting both children. The other option would be to place one of the children with the Welshs and place the other child with another family.

Questions

The author presented an interesting case that leaves you with a difficult decision. Review the work you have done throughout this case and the information he provided, and respond to the following questions. Again, to enhance the learning experience, consider performing these exercises in a small group.

1. List the positives and negatives associated with placing Sarah and Robert together or separately.

2. Based on your work, should Sarah and Robert be placed together or in separate adoptive homes? Explain your reasoning.

3. If Sarah asked you if she could be placed in an adoptive home separate from her brother, would that affect your decision? Please explain.

Once you have finished questions 1 through 3, respond to the following questions to complete the case.

4. Take a moment to review Sarah and Robert's progress in treatment. Based on the author's description, the professional literature, and the latest practice evidence, what occurred to account for their progress, or lack thereof?

5. What was the theoretical approach or combination of approaches that appeared to work best for Sarah and Robert?

6. Based on the work you have done earlier, what additional intervention(s) would you recommend? Use the literature and latest evidence to justify your recommendations.

7. Overall, what is your professional opinion of the work performed in this case? As always, refer to the professional literature, practice evidence, your experience, and the experience of student-colleagues when developing your opinion.

8. Based on this review, what additional or alternative approaches could have been used with this case? That is, if you were the practitioner, how would you have approached this case? Please explain and justify your approach.

9. What did this case demonstrate that you could use in other practice settings? List the most important things you learned by studying this case and how you could use them in your practice career.

Termination, Aftercare, and Follow-Up

Preparing for termination begins early in the treatment process. Proper termination includes many factors, beside how your client progresses in treatment. Hence, this exercise will help you think about the various issues that go into successful termination, aftercare, and follow-up.

Questions

1. Based on your decision regarding placement, list and explain the general factors to consider in developing a successful aftercare plan for Sarah and Robert.

2. List and explain the issues in Sarah and Robert's life to consider when planning for termination and aftercare.

3. What indicators will you use to determine when it is an appropriate time for termination? What does your state law say about aftercare and follow-up in special needs adoption?

4. Plan a specific strategy for termination, aftercare, and follow-up that best fits their reality and professional standards of practice. What does the latest empirical evidence in the field say about these issues?

Evaluation of Practice

Evaluation is important to the practice process. Preparing to evaluate Sarah and Robert's progress in treatment must begin during the early stages of therapy. Evaluative efforts not only allow practitioners to know how their clients are progressing, areas where you need to change your approach, and when it may be appropriate to terminate treatment, but also contribute to the knowledge base of the field and profession. Additionally, most funding sources—private and public—require evidence of practice evaluation and documentation of client outcome. Therefore, developing methods for practice evaluation are essential. Here, this is your task.

Questions

1. Based on your knowledge of research and evaluation methods, develop a plan for practice evaluation that measures both practice process and client outcome.

2. Explain the rationale for your approach and how both targets (process and outcome) are integrated to give an overall evaluation of your practice efforts with Sarah and Robert.

Epilogue

As I was working with Sarah on the adoptive placement, I talked with her about her mutism. The reason Sarah stopped talking was because she believed it was her fault that her mother died. The night of the murder, Sarah and Robert stood at the bottom of the stairs looking up at the fight. When her father was hit by the baseball bat and screamed out in pain, Sarah screamed, and her mother turned to looked down at her from the top of the stairs. At that moment, her father came up behind her mother and cut her throat. Sarah felt that if she had not screamed, her mother would not have looked down at her, and she would be alive.

Bibliography

Bachrach, C., London, K. A., & Maza, P. L. (1991). On the path to adoption: Adoption seeking in the United States. *Journal of Marriage and the Family, 53,* 705–718.

Barth, R. P., & Berry, M. (1988). *Adoption and disruption: Rates, risks, and responses.* New York: Aldine De Gruyter.

Bartholet, E. (1999). *Nobody's children.* Boston: Beacon Press.

Bean, P. (ed.). (1984). *Adoption essays in social policy, law, and sociology.* London: Tavistock Publications.

Berry, M. (1990). Preparing and supporting special needs adoptive families: A review of the literature. *Child and Adolescent Social Work, 7*(5), 403–418.

Brodzinsky, D. M., Lang, R., & Smith, D. W. (1995). Parenting adoptive children. In M. C. Bornstein (ed.), *Handbook of parenting* (pp. 209–232). Hillsdale, NJ: Lawrence Erlbaum Associates, Inc.

Carp, E. W. (1998). *Family matters. Secrecy and disclosure in the history of adoption.* Cambridge, MA: Harvard University Press.

Frasch, K. M., Brooks, D., & Barth, R. P. (2000). Openness and contact in foster care adoptions: An eight-year follow-up. *Family Relations: Interdisciplinary Journal of Applied Family Studies, 45*(4), 435–446.

Grotevant, H. D., McRoy, R. G., Elde, C. L., & Fravel, D. L. (1994). Adoptive family systems dynamics: Variations by level of openness in adoption. *Family Process, 32*(2), 125–146.

Grove, V., & Rosenberg, K. F. (1998). *Clinical and practice issues in adoption: Bridging the gap between adoptees placed as infants and as older children.* Westport, CT: Praeger.

Groze, V. (1996). *Successful adoptive families.* Westport, CT: Praeger.

Hartman, A. (1984). *Working with adoptive families beyond placement.* New York: Child Welfare League of America, Inc.

Howe, D. (1998). *Patterns of adoption: Nature, nurture, and psychosocial development.* Osney Mead, Oxford: Blackwell Science Ltd.

Kadushin, A., & Martin, J. A. (1988). *Child welfare services.* New York: McMillan Publication Co.

McRoy, R. G. (1999). *Special needs adoptions: Practice issues.* New York: Garland Publishing, Inc.

Miall, C. E. (1996). The social construction of adoption: Clinical and community perspectives. *Family Relations, 45,* 301–317.

Mullin, E. S., & Johnson, L. (1999). The role of birth/previously adopted children in families choosing to adopt children with special needs. *Child Welfare, 78*(5), 579–591.

National Adoption Information Clearinghouse (2002). Disruption and dissolution. Retrieved May 9, 2002, from the World Wide Web: http://www.calib.com/ naic/pubs/s_disrup.htm.

Pertman, A. (2000). *Adoption nation: How the adoption revolution is transforming America.* New York: Basic Books.

Priel, B., Melamed-Hass, S., Besser, A., & Kantor, B. (2002). Adjustment among adopted children: The role of maternal self-reflectiveness. *Family Relationships, 49,* 389–396.

Reitz, M., & Watson, K. W. (1992). *Adoption and the family system: Strategies for treatment.* New York: The Guilford Press.

Rosenberg, E. B. (1992). *The adoption life cycle: The children and their families through the years.* New York. The Free Press.

Stein, L. M., & Hoopes, J. L. (1985). *Identity formation in the adopted adolescent.* New York: Child Welfare League of America.

Terrell, J., & Modell, J. (1994). Anthropology and adoption. *American Anthropologist, 96*(1), 155–161.

Watson, K. W. (1996, November). Family-centered adoption practice. *Families in Society: The Journal of Contemporary Human Services, 77*(9), 523–534.

Wierzbicki, M. (1993). Psychological adjustment of adoptees: A meta-analysis. *Journal of Clinical Child Psychology, 22,* 447–454.

United States Department of Health and Human Services. (2002). *Adoption 2002 Executive Summary.*

3

The Morgan Family

Mildred Drollinger & Jill C. Tyler-Skinner

Introduction

Children adopted as infants often experience intensified and exaggerated identity crises during adolescence. Hence, these children often develop significant behavioral problems that require professional assistance. The following case study describes one adoptive family's experience in counseling provided through a home-based intervention program at a non-profit social service agency in the Midwest. The service is a family preservation program that assists adoptive families in crisis utilizing a multi-systemic approach. The program began in 1994 with a contract between the agency and the local County Public Welfare Agency. In 1996, the program received the Innovative Program of the Year award from a statewide non-profit child welfare organization.

Meeting the Morgan Family: Presenting Problem

The county social services adoption monitor, a social worker who follows adoption cases until the child becomes an adult, referred the Morgan family to our Post Adoption Support Services program. The monitor believed that the Morgan family needed counseling because of problems with their oldest son, Devon. The monitor stated that Mr. and Mrs. Morgan did not know how to help Devon overcome his behavioral and attitude problems. Devon was a 15-year-old boy who, according to the monitor and the Morgans, had exhibited serious behavioral and attitude problems over the last year.

The family consisted of Mr. and Mrs. Morgan; Devon; Robert, age 13; and Hannah, age 9. Mr. Morgan was a supervisor at the post office and worked the third shift. Mrs. Morgan was a stay-at-home mother who also provided childcare for two neighbor children in the family home three days per week. As a Caucasian middle class family, the Morgans resided in a rural area about 30 miles from the city. They participated in a small, Protestant church. Both claimed that their faith was important to the family. Devon's refusal to attend church suggested to the Morgans that he lacked conscience. Because they lived in a small community, Mr. and Mrs. Morgan knew that many people knew about Devon's problems. For his part, Devon hated living in a small community. He claimed that "there was nothing to do." In reality, many local teens went to the city for entertainment.

Mrs. Morgan was a quiet, sensitive woman who tried to please everyone in the family. Mr. Morgan worked hard but often made critical remarks about his wife, at home and in public. He could be a "difficult" person to live with. It is important to note that Mr. Morgan had a repaired cleft palate and cleft lip and a noticeable speech impediment.

The Morgans adopted Devon when he was four months old. They had always wanted a family but were unable to have children of their own. However, as sometimes happens, after adopting Devon, the Morgans proceeded to have two biological children. According to Mr. and Mrs. Morgan, Devon's current problems began one year earlier. He began lying about "everything," stealing (including his parents' credit cards), breaking into neighbors' homes, arguing with his younger siblings, and being defiant, especially to his mother. In addition, Devon refused to do household chores or attend church with the family. Moreover, Mrs. Morgan believed that Devon had experimented with marijuana and alcohol and she wondered what effect this had on his behavior and attitude.

When we met, Devon was in the tenth grade at a local high school. His parents said that Devon had difficulty learning, unless he could experience his lessons "hands-on." According to his parents, Devon's grades were "mediocre" and he had always presented his teachers many social challenges. That is, Devon's problems in school dated to kindergarten. Teachers frequently complained that Devon was disruptive, lacked discipline, and would not follow through with school-related activities. Hence, when Devon was 10 years old, the school social worker and psychologist diagnosed him with Attention Deficit Hyperactive Disorder (ADHD). When counseling began, Devon took Ritalin for his disorder.

In his leisure time, Devon enjoyed listening to music and using the computer. He also participated in soccer and track at school. Devon had a few friends at school but was not especially close to any of them. He liked being alone and seemed able to occupy his time without needing people around. Yet, Mr. and Mrs. Morgan believed that Devon "should" be with friends more often. They worried about him.

Questions

The authors offered introductory information about Devon and his family as they prepared to undergo counseling. Based on what you have read so far, respond to the following questions before moving ahead with this case.

1. What is your first hunch regarding the presenting problem? Explore the practice literature about post-adoption issues and discuss your findings with other students. What is the prevalence of post-adoptive problems in adolescents adopted as infants? If the literature does not speak specifically about this problem, are there other problems or categories of problems that this behavior fits with pertaining to treatment?

2. What is your next direction of inquiry and assessment? Further, explore the practice literature to locate theories or models that apply to this type of behavior in adolescent boys. Based on your findings, what information do you need to perform a comprehensive multi-systemic assessment? (See Chapter 1).

3. Make a preliminary list of Devon and the family's problems and strengths.

4. Since the family stated that faith was important to them, does Devon's refusal to attend church with the family have any significance?

Multi-Systemic Assessment Process

I provided the information above to introduce you to the Morgan family and describe the problems that brought them into treatment at my agency. I collected most of that information from the referral source and through a telephone conversation with Mrs. Morgan prior to our first meeting.

Below, I discuss the process used to engage the family in therapy. My main task as the practitioner in our post-adoption support program was to help the adoptive family stay together. Most adoption agencies provide this type of ongoing support to adoptive families as they struggle with issues related to adoption. It was clear from my initial conversation with Mrs. Morgan that they hoped that therapy would "fix" Devon. As many clients do, the Morgans believed that therapy worked similar to "magic." That is, clients often enter therapy under the impression that practitioners will come up with some intervention that makes their problems disappear. My job was to change that mindset; to help clients understand that problems only subside through a process that includes hard work.

Mrs. Morgan's next statement made the reason for the referral to our program clear. Mrs. Morgan stated emphatically that if Devon did not change his behavior, they wanted him placed in foster care. She said that they were "tired" of fighting with Devon, and that their other two children were "suffering" because of Devon's "bad attitude." While they agreed that Devon needed to change, Mrs. Morgan said that she and her husband disagreed on how to handle Devon. Mrs. Morgan was the "easier" parent and Mr. Morgan tried to be a strict disciplinarian. She thought that he was too strict. During our telephone conversation, I explained the program and set an appointment to meet the family at the Morgan home for their convenience.

Having previously spoken to Mrs. Morgan, when I arrived at their house I made a special point to introduce myself to Mr. Morgan. I also quickly introduced myself to each child. As I entered their comfortable and spacious house, I sensed the usual air of tension. However, I also sensed that the Morgans were determined to help Devon, meaning that engaging the parents in treatment might be easier than engaging Devon. Normally, when they are considered the "problem," adolescents are difficult to engage in therapy. Devon was no exception. I asked him to join the session, knowing that he probably had "more important" things to do with his time than attend counseling. Devon laughed, but agreed to stay. Mrs. Morgan prepared coffee and cookies. I complimented her about the hospitality and on their home and yard. I also commented on a recent newspaper article about their community's local school. I wanted them to know that I paid attention to them.

I completed my assessment over two sessions at the Morgans' home. At the beginning of our first session, I collected basic demographic information about each family member, beginning with Mr. Morgan. I made a special point to ask each person to discuss his or her personal interests and hobbies. This always helps create a relaxed and comfortable atmosphere for conversation. I moved my focus from person to person around the living room, asking everyone to talk at length about his or her life.

Sharing Personal Information

When this phase of the session finished and before moving into serious inquiry, I offered the family some personal background information. I discussed my education and experience with adoptive families. Additionally, I briefly mentioned that I was a parent of adoptive children who had behavioral problems as teenagers. This seemed to relax the Morgans.

I am always careful about sharing this information. As an adoptive parent who raised children with problems similar to Devon's, I strived for balance between empowering parents and not over identifying with them, especially if I wanted to engage Devon. I let Mr. and Mrs. Morgan know that I understood their experience but also tried to help them understand that their son, in the process of finding his identity, was "hurting" too. Devon had reasons for acting as he did, even if he could not say them aloud. I suggested that Devon wanted boundaries and, in fact, his behavior suggested that he wanted stricter parents. Devon gave his parents the message that he wanted independence and the freedom to make his own decisions. Paradoxically, he felt out of control and wanted his parents to provide more structure. I also believed, but did not say it aloud, that Devon might be testing their commitment to him because he was not their birth child.

Questions

As longtime practitioners and social work educators, the editors find that what, when, if, and how much practitioners should share about their lives with clients always generates interesting dialogue and debate. Some believe that sharing personal information is a way of joining clients as well as being genuine in the relationship. Others believe that practitioners should not share personal information with clients under any circumstances. This interesting debate is relevant in every aspect of practice.

1. Explore the practice literature about client engagement, relationship building, and practitioner use of self in practice. Explore these topics either alone or in the context of two or three different theoretical approaches of interest. What does the literature say about professional use of self, defined as sharing personal information with clients? If there are differences between approaches or models, how do authors account for their beliefs about this issue?

2. Explore the code of professional ethics (NASW, 2000). What does the code say, if anything, about this issue? List the various standards that might inform practitioners about this issue and come to a decision about its ethicality in practice.

3. If you decide that it is appropriate to share personal information, when and under what circumstances is it appropriate?

4. If you decide that it is inappropriate to share personal information, explain and defend your position.

5. Discuss this issue with classmates. Perhaps you could have a formal debate in class about this issue as part of your research and decision-making process.

The Interview

I used a problem-oriented family interview to assess the Morgans. This interview format helped determine each person's perspectives and views about the family situation and de-emphasized Devon as the identified client. The Morgans were unusual in one way. They had a traditional marriage that allowed Mrs. Morgan to remain home with the children. Mr. Morgan's income was sufficient to meet the family's financial needs. To assess their beliefs and feelings about their relationship, I said that in most families I work with, both parents usually work outside the home. They reacted to this comment with pride. Mrs. Morgan said that she wanted to "be there" for the children, especially when they returned from school. She also enjoyed the freedom she had as a homemaker. She volunteered at their church and spent time with her friends. She earned extra money by taking care of the neighbor's two children. However, she found it more important to help her neighbors than earn money. Mrs. Morgan was proud of her role as homemaker and demonstrated this by providing refreshments when I visited their home.

Regarding parenting, Mr. and Mrs. Morgan readily shared that they had differing parenting styles. Mrs. Morgan admitted that she tended to yell at the children, sometimes saying more than she needed. She often lost her temper and regretted saying harsh things to Devon in the "heat of the moment." Mr. Morgan said that he simply "said what he had to say" to the children before walking away, taking a "matter-of-fact" approach to the kids. When I complimented his ability to do this, Mrs. Morgan said that he had not always been so calm. In fact, she stated that he used to have a worse temper then her. While he never hit the children, Mr. Morgan could "raise the roof" when he became angry.

Mrs. Morgan claimed that her husband changed how he related to the children because of his involvement in Promise Keeper retreats for men. She said that he began changing after Promise Keepers emphasized his spiritual responsibility to his family. He interpreted that to mean less anger and stricter rules. He (and his wife) believed that as the father, he was "in charge" of the family and could not afford to be emotional and angry. It seemed that Mr. Morgan took this message to heart related to child discipline.

I asked the couple to provide an example of their different parenting styles. When Devon stole their credit card, Mr. Morgan wanted to press charges against Devon. Mrs. Morgan disagreed because she feared that pressing charges would give Devon a juvenile record that would harm him later in life. Both reported that they never directly resolved their disagreement. Indirectly (they never discussed it), they resolved the issue by not pressing charges. In fact, the Morgans did not formally respond to the incident, beyond scolding and futile attempts to ground Devon.

The Morgans reported few problems with their two younger children. Both Robert and Hannah were smart children who received excellent grades. Mrs. Morgan said that Robert and Devon got along better, as Robert grew older. However, Devon and Hannah did not get along. Mrs. Morgan said that she spent a lot of time managing their feisty relationship.

Rapport with Devon

Now that I had heard from the Morgans about their problems with Devon, I wanted to hear from Devon. At first, he refused to speak. To motivate adolescents to participate, I asked each family member to discuss how he or she viewed the problems in the family. Since everyone talked about Devon, it did not take him long to speak on his own behalf.

Devon believed that his parents treated him differently than his siblings. He wanted his parents to become stricter with his siblings. He said that his parents were easier on them because Robert and Hannah were "their" kids and stricter with him because he was "adopted." When I told Devon that I could help his parents become stricter, he took a more active role in the session. I took advantage of his concern and agreed with him that parents needed to be in charge of their home and family, which in turn helped to empower his parents. When his parents agreed that they needed help parenting Devon, he injected that they needed help parenting the other kids too. Devon said that he wasn't as "bad" as everyone said, and he denied using drugs or drinking. He said that he was just "growing up" and wanted his parents to give him more independence. He was "15 after all," and did not need his parents treating him as if he was a "baby."

The parents responded as parents often do when their adolescents make this statement. Mr. Morgan said that as long as Devon kept acting like a baby, they would keep treating him as one. He told Devon that they would treat him as he treated them. If he acted like a 10 year old, they would treat him as a 10 year old.

To underscore the strengths of the family, I shifted from discussing problems to strengths. I asked each to list what they liked most about being members of their family. I was amazed that they found few things worth discussing. They struggled to find anything positive in their lives. This is common in families experiencing problems. Sometimes, families focus so much on their problems that they forget to notice what they liked about the family. This usually indicates that families lack hope for a positive future.

Devon had to leave to meet a friend, but I had one more question for him. Because Devon was adopted, I asked him if he wanted to know more about his birth family. Devon answered with a resounding, "No."

After Devon left, I excused the other children and met briefly with the Morgans alone. They struggled with the idea that the family had to be in counseling since Devon was the obvious problem. I explained the benefits of family therapy over individual therapy for Devon; that because most teenagers are self-centered and resent authority, they view their parents as the problem. Furthermore, Devon, like most teenagers, was not a good candidate for individual change. I explained that as the Morgans changed the way they handled Devon, his behavior might improve. Without the family, we had little hope for changing Devon. Both Mr. and Mrs. Morgan commented on Devon's participation during the session. I complimented them on their ability to endure a challenging child.

Questions

The author provided more information about the Morgans. Before moving on in the case, respond to the following questions based on the information provided so far.

1. The author asked Devon if he wanted to know about his birth parents. Explore the relevant professional literature to locate information pertaining to this issue in post-adoptive treatment. Based on that information and your experience, do you believe it was appropriate to ask Devon about his birth parents in the first session? If so, please explain. If not, when (if ever) should practitioners address this issue?

2. Based on the limited information you have to this point and your examination of the literature, discuss your hunch about Devon's reasons for saying no to learning about his birth family.

3. Devon's interest in the session seemed to peak when the author discussed helping Mr. and Mrs. Morgan; based on your knowledge of this and other post-adoptive cases, what hunches do you have about the meaning of his interest? Based on your hunch, what further information do you need to investigate your hunch to see if it is correct?

4. What further information do you need at this point to complete a genogram for this family? How would you go about gathering this information? Discuss these issues with classmates. You may want to role-play a session with this family to practice collecting family-based information.

I observed an interesting dynamic between Mr. and Mrs. Morgan. Several times, Mr. Morgan talked to his wife in a demeaning way. For example, when Mrs. Morgan mentioned that she might be too easy on the children, I suggested that I could help her become firmer with the kids. Mr. Morgan commented, "That'll be the day." Mr. Morgan interjected comments such as this throughout the session, sometimes even generating laughter from the kids. Mrs. Morgan ignored him, but I could tell from her facial expression and shrinking body posture that she did not like it. However, she never commented on his sarcastic and demeaning comments. I found this interesting, especially since one of the Morgan's major complaints about Devon and, to a lesser extent Robert and Hannah, was the demeaning way the children spoke to their mother.

Toward the end of the first session, I summarized the areas the family wanted to change. Mr. Morgan wanted Mrs. Morgan to become firmer with Devon. Devon wanted his parents to become as strict with the younger children as they were toward him. Mr. and Mrs. Morgan wanted Devon's acting out and negative attitude to cease or they would place him in foster care. Hannah wanted Devon to be nicer to her, and Robert thought things in the family were fine the way they were.

I encouraged Mr. and Mrs. Morgan to present a united front as parents. That is, before disciplining the children, the parents should privately agree on a course of action and support each other when the children objected. In addition, I also encouraged Mr. and Mrs. Morgan to take care of their marriage by going on "dates" without the children. I emphasized that this was important to work on now, because eventually the kids would leave home, leaving them alone with each other.

I asked the family to sign a release of information form so that I could obtain Devon's previous records and a copy of their original adoption family assessment. I left Initial Progress Evaluation Scales for the parents to complete on themselves and Devon. The scales help parents examine their parenting skills and provide information about Mr. and Mrs. Morgan's perceptions of their son. The scales measured parental cooperation and involvement, motivation for problem solving, use of physical punishment and verbal discipline, the parents' mental health, and the family's support system. The progress evaluation scales for Devon focused on individual behavior. The scales measured Devon's family interactions, school attendance, getting along with others, feelings and mood, use of free time, behavioral problems, and attitude. I intended to reuse the evaluation scales at termination to measure the family's progress.

Ongoing Assessment

Assessment is an ongoing process, not a static event (Johnson, 2004). Hence, I continued assessing the Morgan family in future sessions. For example, during the next session, I asked Mr. and Mrs. Morgan to share information about their family-of-origin. Specifically I was interested in learning about their parents as well as information about their current relationships with extended family members. I used a genogram to obtain information. This tool assisted Mr. and Mrs. Morgan in evaluating their own parenting styles and helped me understand their social support system.

Mr. Morgan's Family-of-Origin

Mr. Morgan grew up as the oldest of three children. He stated that his father was a "hard worker" with a "violent" temper. He drank and would often take his frustrations out on his wife and the kids. Mr. Morgan's memories of childhood revolved around his father's temper and his fear that his father would hit him if he did not follow orders. He said that his father was not "abusive," but that he was "spanked" with a belt when he "messed up." He remains in contact with his siblings, although they were not "close." His father died several years earlier and his mother lived near the Morgan home. She often served as the family babysitter.

Mrs. Morgan's Family-of-Origin

Interestingly, it sounded as if Mrs. Morgan grew up in the same family. She also had two younger sisters and a "violent" father. She described her mother as a "saintly" woman who managed to keep the family together and "happy," despite her father's drinking, loudness, and violent temper. She said that her house was "loud" and "chaotic" as a child, and she remembers many nights listening to her father yell and scream at her mother. While she did not want to define her father as "abusive," she did say that he slapped and hit her mother often.

Sibling Rivalry?

As the Morgans became comfortable, I inquired about the relationship between Devon and his younger siblings. Devon appeared to feel different, even jealous of the birth status of his siblings. His feelings affected his interactions with all family members. For some reason, Devon reacted strongest to Hannah. Perhaps, he reacted to her because she was the youngest. Devon also said that he believed Hannah was Mr. and Mrs. Morgan's "favorite" child. Robert agreed, but did not seem to mind.

Robert and Devon had a normal sibling relationship. Hannah was the "typical" younger sister that "tattled" on Devon, even attempting to give orders. Devon would threaten her and Hannah would scream for her mother. I observed that all of the Morgan children had explosive tempers that flared often and quickly.

Questions

Now that the author has presented more information about Devon and his family, perform the following exercises based on your education, experience, the professional literature, and the available best practice evidence. To increase your learning potential, you may want to do this in a small group with other students in your course.

1. Based on the information contained above, construct a three-generation genogram and eco-map that represents Devon's personal, familial, and environmental circumstances. What further information do you need to complete this exercise? What patterns do these two important graphical assessment tools demonstrate?

2. Building on your earlier work, complete a list of Devon's problems and strengths, drawing from multi-systemic sources.

3. Write a two- to three-page narrative assessment that encompasses Devon's multi-systemic issues and strengths. Review Chapter 1 if needed. This narrative should provide a comprehensive and multi-systemic explanation of their life as the Morgans prepare to undergo therapy with the author. Below we offer a few questions to guide this process:

- **What are your hunches regarding Devon's view of himself as a son and developing young man?**
- **What are your hunches about his feelings regarding his adolescent identity and his status as the only adopted child in this family?**
- **What are your hunches regarding his ability to be honest in his relationship with his parents?**
- **What are your hunches about the role Devon's adoption plays in this family's presentation?**

4. Try to identify the theoretical model or approach that you use to guide your assessment. According to the literature, what other theoretical options are available and how would these change the nature of your assessment?

5. End by developing multi-axial DSM-IV-TR diagnoses for both Devon and his family. Provide a list of client symptoms that you used to justify your diag-

nostic decision. What, if any, information was missing that would make this an easier task?

6. The author used several evaluation scales to assess the family's skills, attitudes, and daily functioning and to help measure progress in therapy over time. Explore the professional literature and locate three different family or individual evaluation scales. Examine their efficacy with adoptive families. Based on the literature and your experience, would you use these scales in work with clients? Explain your opinions.

Treatment Planning

After meeting twice with the Morgan family, we decided on a treatment plan designed to address their problems, making it possible for the family to remain together. The Morgans agreed to work on the following issues in therapy:

1. *Parenting Skills and Relationship.* The Morgans agreed that they needed to learn effective strategies for dealing with their children, including improving their ability to work together to solve problems. They also agreed to work on their communication style between each other and between parents and children. Both parents wanted the family to be less sarcastic and hostile in the way they communicated.
2. *Devon's Behavior and Attitude.* The Morgans agreed that Devon needed to change his behaviors or they would move to have him placed in temporary foster care of a residential program for troubled teenagers. Devon disagreed that he needed to change.

Treatment Approach

I used a variety of treatment models with the Morgans including crisis intervention (Aguilera, 1998; Turner, 1996), reality therapy, communication therapy (Turner, 1996), problem-solving therapy (Haley, 1987), and solution-focused therapy (De Jong & Berg, 2002). I primarily used a solution-focused approach with the family. I provided services in the family home and at Devon's school where I often met Devon and his school counselor. Overall, my task was to help the Morgans stay together and keep Devon at home with his adoptive parents.

I arranged weekly family therapy sessions with the Morgans. Devon and I met individually after each family session. The family therapy sessions had two parts. I met first with the whole family, then with Mr. and Mrs. Morgan as a couple. After three sessions, Devon began skipping appointments. He showed up approximately every third session. When Devon missed sessions, we kept meeting as a family. I hoped that Devon would return to our weekly schedule, or the Morgans would reach the point where they could insist that he attend.

In addition to formal therapy, I also incorporated education into our work. We discussed normal adolescent development, parenting, adoption issues, and other systems in the community such as the juvenile justice system. For additional support, I invited the Morgans to participate in our agency's monthly adoptive parent support group.

Questions

In his work pertaining to families and family therapy, Jay Haley (1980) stated that a family's presenting symptoms, particularly when children were the presenting problem, usually represented a metaphor for other, sometimes more significant issues in the family. He claimed that understanding the metaphoric meaning of a family's presenting problems provided practitioners with valuable clues about overall family functioning and can provide clues about possible intervention planning with families. In the exercise below, use this approach to look at Devon in the context of his family.

1. Locate and read Haley's ideas pertaining to the meaning of symptoms in family assessment and treatment.

2. Develop a list of possible metaphors that define Devon's presenting problem related to himself, adolescent development, and/or his family system.

3. Compare the treatment plan you established above with the author's treatment plan. What differences and similarities exist between the plans? How do you account for the differences? Use the professional literature and practice evidence to analyze both plans, and the differences between them.

4. Develop a revised treatment plan from information provided by the author, your original plan, and the practice literature. What does the evidenced-based practice literature say are the most effective ways to treat clients with the Morgan's problems and strengths? Using the rationale from the literature and your experience, develop a position on this issue.

Course of Treatment

Parenting Styles

Among the many problems they had, Mrs. Morgan worried most about her inability to handle the children's behavior (especially Devon) when Mr. Morgan was at work. Since he worked third shift, Mrs. Morgan spent every night dealing with the children alone. Mr. Morgan would try to help by disciplining the children before he left for work, leaving her to follow through overnight. She recalled several nights when Mr. Morgan ordered the children to their rooms for acting out, expecting the kids to remain in their rooms the entire evening. Once he left for work, the children would leave their rooms and challenge their mother to do something about it. Mrs. Morgan usually "begged" them to return to their rooms by threatening to tell their father when he got home the next morning.

The parents agreed that they might be more effective if they made the children remain in their rooms for a shorter period. Mr. and Mrs. Morgan decided together that the kids would have shorter time outs, no longer than 30 minutes. Mrs. Morgan would set a timer. They also agreed that once the time out ended, Mrs. Morgan would not mention it again. After trying this a few times, Mrs. Morgan said that she was successful and it made her feel more in control. I also asked Mrs. Morgan to read *Parenting Teens with Love and Logic* (Cline & Fay, 1992). She would read a chapter and discuss it with her husband and me. This activity helped the Morgans to begin acting in ways that forced Devon to become more responsible for his own actions, a major concern for her husband.

Devon helped by providing the parents with a chance to practice their new skills. For example, one night Devon was determined to go to an out-of-town concert without his parents' permission. Mr. and Mrs. Morgan decided there was no way to stop him from going. Hence, they agreed to force him up in the morning for school, regardless of how tired he was, or how much trouble he gave them. When the following morning arrived, the parents woke Devon and forced him off to school, ignoring his pleas for more sleep.

As the Morgans and I discussed adolescent development, Mr. and Mrs. Morgan wondered if Devon's behaviors were normal adolescent behavior or symptoms of bigger problems. I suggested that it was a complicated issue. Certainly, there were a number of factors that could have played roles in Devon's behavior, including his age, adoption issues, his ADHD, peer pressure, and/or his unique personality. We discussed how much things had changed for teenagers since the Morgans were young. The Morgans wanted to find a single reason for Devon's behavior, but they were learning that it was not that simple.

Questions

It is always difficult for parents and professionals alike to know when a teenager's behavior represents normal adolescent experimentation or is symptomatic of bigger problems. This subject comes up in work with adolescents and families in every practice setting. Therefore, it is an important issue to consider.

1. Explore the professional practice literature to find information about this subject. What does the literature say about normal adolescent behavior, especially for adolescents adopted as children?

2. As you read Devon's case, what aspects of his behavior were normal for an adopted adolescent? What aspects of his behavior were related to his family systems environment?

Working on Their Marriage

The Morgans wanted to improve their communication and work on their marriage. I worked with the couple on communication exercises and provided reading material. They learned active listening and reflective skills to help each communicate better with the other. I also assigned activities they could try at home between sessions. Both partners seemed to work hard at improving their ability to communicate, especially around parenting issues.

The couple also agreed with Devon that they needed more time together as a couple, without the children present. However, they did not trust Devon. Both believed that he simply wanted them out of the house so he could have his friends over. I complimented them on seeing that this could be part of Devon's plan, but suggested that it was still a good idea. The couple spent time figuring out when they could find time for each other given their busy schedules and Mr. Morgan's third-shift schedule. Finally, they agreed to go out alone while the kids were in school. When this went well, the Morgans decided to go away for a few days. They asked a grandmother to watch Devon at her house while they were gone. While Devon was not overly excited, he agreed and remained at his grandmother's house while the Morgans vacationed alone.

Temper Tantrums

The Morgans were troubled about the loud, angry, and sarcastic ways that the family interacted. I observed that all of the kids had quick and loud temper tantrums when they did not get their way. I also noticed that Mr. Morgan treated his wife similarly. While he no longer yelled, he was quietly sarcastic and demeaning. This pattern ran through the entire family system, beginning in each parent's family-of-origin. That is, their interaction style represented an intergenerational pattern.

As a family, we discussed the disruption that constant temper tantrums caused, and that perhaps everyone could learn to control their anger. Although she often yelled at the kids, Mrs. Morgan was relatively calm. Moreover, Devon's temper was mild compared to his younger siblings. For everyone's sake, it was helpful to find an issue where Devon was not the problem. Mr. Morgan shared that his childhood family was chaotic because of his father's temper. He said that he always wanted a quieter home when he grew up.

To address this issue, I asked the family to keep track of their temper outbursts for one week. At the next session, the family proudly reported that they had fewer outbursts. A discussion followed regarding ways to better control their tempers, and I pointed out that this might be something they have to work on for a while. Simply asking the family to record temper tantrums helped the family reduce the number and intensity of the tantrums. I asked them to continue recording temper tantrums in search of a familial pattern that we could explore later, if needed.

I also used their genogram to help the Morgans explore their family-of-origin issues and patterns. They spent at least two sessions recalling the hostility of their upbringing. Mrs. Morgan finally admitted that her father abused her mother. She also revealed that she used to be afraid of her husband. Although he never hit her, his tone and anger made her think of her father. For his part, Mr. Morgan admitted that he joined Promise Keepers because his temper scared him. He stated that he decided to address his temper before he lost control and took his anger out on his kids or wife, as his father did in his family. They ultimately understood that their family repeated the patterns they (the parents) learned growing up, despite their personal desires to be different.

Devon's Individual Therapy

My individual session with Devon proceeded in a normal fashion. Devon was mainly interested in finding ways to keep his parents "off his back." Over time, I noticed that Devon's poor self-image interfered with his ability to make positive choices and often dictated his responses to his parents. I began wondering what effect his adoptive status in a family with two biological children had on his self-identity.

Devon also had trouble processing and verbalizing his thoughts. On more than one occasion when we were talking, Devon said, "I'm not getting it." Even with repeated attempts to explain concepts, Devon struggled. He became easily frustrated and would respond defiantly, often with obscene language. When I questioned him further about this, Devon finally admitted that he often did not understand what teachers said in school. He would respond by putting his head down on the desk. Devon admitted feeling "bored and depressed" about his life and worried that he was "slow." In typical adolescent logic, Devon believed that the only way his life would improve was by getting his driver's license and a job.

I tried to engage Devon around the issue of behavioral choices and consequences. He was not going for it. All Devon focused on was how he could obtain his driver's license and become more independent. Devon said he wanted to move away from home to live in his "own place." I encouraged Devon to explore how much it would cost per month to have his own apartment. Soon, he dropped that line of discussion entirely. I think he discovered that a 15-year-old high school sophomore could not afford an apartment.

Devon also shared his frustration regarding interactions with his younger sister. According to Devon, Hannah would whisper smart remarks to him and then scream for her mother's help when Devon responded. I spent time discussing better ways for Devon to deal with Hannah. I also encouraged him to bring this up during a family session.

An Ethical Dilemma

After we discussed confidentiality, during one of our individual sessions Devon talked about his friends and their activities, including their alcohol and other drug use. Devon admitted that he smoked marijuana and drank with friends. He said that he had a "high tolerance" for alcohol and drank a lot, sometimes as much as 10 or 12 cans of beer, and/or several shots of liquor. He said that he did not have a drinking problem because he didn't "need" to drink. He also told me that he was sexually active. When I asked him what he wanted to do with this information, he replied, "Please snitch on me. I give you permission to snitch on me."

I found myself in a dilemma. While I thought that Mr. and Mrs. Morgan should know about these issues, I also thought it was important for Devon to trust me. I decided not to tell the Morgans about Devon's substance abuse and sexual activity. Instead, I discussed how many teenagers experiment with alcohol, drugs, and sex at Devon's age. I did find it curious that Devon wanted me to "snitch" on him, but he would not tell his parents about his own activities. I encouraged Devon to tell his parents during a family session. To my knowledge, this never happened.

Questions

The author decided to withhold information from the Morgans about their son's substance abuse and sexual behavior. She decided that the relationship with Devon forbade her from informing the parents about these issues. Some would agree with the author's interpretation of relationships, while others might say that she had an obligation to inform Devon's parents about his activities. While trust is always a dilemma when working with teenagers, how far should practitioners go to maintain trust when they are working in a family context? Based on the information in this case, please respond to the following questions.

1. Explore the professional literature pertaining to confidentiality and its limits. Also, explore the code of professional ethics (NASW, 2000). Based on your findings, do you agree with how the author handled this situation? Do confidentiality rules and regulations force practitioners to withhold information between adolescents and parents? What are the limits of confidentiality in social work practice? Explain your answer in the context of the code of ethics and confidentiality rules and regulations.

2. Do practitioners have the right to withhold information from parents in situations such as this? Remember to consider the clinical context in which the author worked with Devon and the family. Does that change your opinion about this situation?

3. Discuss this issue with classmates, colleagues, or people at your field practicum site. What is the consensus of other professionals about how you should handle this situation when it occurs in your practice career?

Adoption Issues

As Devon and I became better acquainted, I believed that Devon's behavioral problems related to an intensified and exaggerated identity crisis stemming from his adoption. The presence of his two siblings exaggerated Devon's negative feelings. Robert and Hannah were the Morgans biological children, and Devon believed that his parents loved them more than him. He also believed that they wanted to rid themselves of him. In response to his feelings and beliefs, and in an effort to fit in with his peers, Devon rebelled.

Objectively, I disagreed with Devon's opinion about his parents. I believed that Mr. and Mrs. Morgan loved Devon and that his adoptive status did not cause them to treat him differently. The Morgans treated him differently because he presented so many problems in the family. Yet, Devon could not escape his feelings about being "different." Robert and Hannah did not have learning problems or ADHD. Additionally, Devon looked different. Except for dark hair (a family commonality), Devon had finer features than the rest of the family and he was much taller than everyone else. At 15 years old, Devon was already 6′ tall while his father was only 5′7″. Despite these differences, I believed that Devon was a "Morgan," just as Robert and Hannah were Morgans. However, Devon's feelings are common, especially among adopted teenagers.

Interest in His Birth Family

During our first session some weeks earlier, Devon emphatically denied any interest in learning about his birth family. However, during an individual session, Devon asked if it was possible to locate his birth parents. I said that it was, and explained our state's law regarding locating birth parents. It turned out that Devon had secretly wanted to know about his birth parents for some time. For example, during a session Mr. Morgan offered to show me a letter written to the family by the agency shortly after they adopted Devon. In this letter, the agency described Devon's birth family and the reason they gave Devon up for adoption. However, Mr. Morgan could not find the letter. It was missing from their file. He calmly asked Devon if he had the letter. He did. Yet, Devon told his father that he did not want to know anything about his original parents.

Devon's ambivalence about his birth parents was common. On the one hand, Devon wanted information about them. Perhaps he was looking to understand why his parents gave him up for adoption. Maybe he was interested in knowing them. Alternatively, Devon would not admit his curiosity in front of the Morgans. Most likely, he did not want to hurt his adoptive parents or have them believe that he did not love them. Adopted children face this dilemma every day. They live with a sense of missing identity, of not knowing who they are or why their original parents "did not want" them. This is why I believe adopted children should learn about their birth parents. However, this should only happen when they (adopted children) are ready and able to handle the information. When we worked together, Devon was curious, but not ready to announce his intentions to learn about this aspect of his life. I sensed that the Morgans would support his curiosity. Devon would have to "cross that bridge" when he was ready.

Questions

1. Explore the professional literature on adoption. Based on your inquiry, can you explain Devon's ambivalence about his birth parents?

2. What significance did his taking the agency letter have for Devon?

3. What are the rules surrounding finding birth parents in your state? Given these rules and the nature of adoption in your state, what is your opinion about Devon's apparent desire to learn about his birth parents? If you were Devon's therapist, how would you handle this situation? Be sure to consider the potential affects of your strategy on his adoptive family.

Legal Troubles

Two months into our treatment, I learned that Devon had stolen his mother's car for a "joy ride" at least twice. Mrs. Morgan awoke one night to find Devon and her car missing. She immediately called the police and reported the car stolen. On this occasion, both parents agreed that pressing charges was appropriate. The Morgans became frustrated when the local sheriff's office did not take the situation seriously. Two months later Devon appeared in Juvenile Court and received a $50.00 fine. Fortunately, the hearing officer took the offense seriously. He warned Devon that he was to pay the fine, not his parents. In addition, the officer told Devon that if he stole the car again, he would lose his right to a driver's license until he was 19 years old. I was at the hearing and saw Devon in tears.

Six months later, Devon found himself in trouble again. This time he had skipped school with a friend. They broke into a home and stole money, cigarettes, and cigarette lighters. The police charged Devon with breaking and entering. Shortly before they learned about this offense, Devon had called to make an appointment. During our session, Devon did not mention the incident. Mrs. Morgan believed that Devon made the appointment because he was concerned about what would happen to him and he wanted me to help him out of trouble.

The second arrest seemed to have a positive affect. Devon began making progress at home and in school. He started telling his parents when he was leaving the house and began coming home on time. His grades also improved and he was easier to get along with at home. It seemed that Devon worried about his future.

This did not last. Devon and a friend had a minor car accident while skipping school. Interestingly enough, Mrs. Morgan came upon the accident shortly after it occurred. Mr. Morgan was angry and contacted me, saying that he wanted Devon placed in a foster home. When I told him that this was not possible, Mr. Morgan became angry. He could not believe that Devon's behavior did not warrant foster care, residential care, or detention. Later in the day, Mr. Morgan called again. He had calmed down considerably. Mr. Morgan said that he had a friend who would give Devon a job. I thought this was a good idea, and supported Mr. Morgan's efforts to help Devon.

His parents did not want Devon to obtain a driver's license until he proved that he was mature enough to handle the responsibility. After much conversation, they finally agreed that it was important for Devon to learn how to drive properly. Therefore, the Morgans allowed Devon to take driver's education, but not to get his license until further notice.

Mr. Morgan continued to insist that it would be better for Devon and the family if Devon were in foster care or detention. Mr. Morgan had a difficult time dealing with Devon's "coming and going as he pleased" and felt unable to do anything about it. He became angry with me on two occasions and verbalized his frustration. He said that if he could use corporal punishment, Devon would not have these problems. Mr. Morgan believed that Devon needed a good "whooping" occasionally to teach him a lesson. Although his anger seemed directed at me, I knew that he was frustrated with his inability to handle Devon. In the end, he agreed that detention or foster care were inappropriate for Devon. They finally faced the fact that Devon was their son to parent, and they could not pass him off to the system.

As a parent of adoptive children, I had a difficult time listening to the Morgan's frustration about not getting the help they wanted. I privately agreed that it might help to have Devon placed in a residential setting. However, there was no funding available for Devon's placement. While I did not like making decisions based on available funding, I also believed that there were disadvantages to having Devon placed in foster care, residential care, or juvenile detention. This would have solidified Devon's place as the "problem" in the family. Other youth would also likely negatively influence him because most of the children in these settings have more severe problems. I believed that the best long-term solution involved in-home care with Devon living at home. However, I also related to their need for a short-term "fix."

Questions

1. Take a moment to review Devon's and the Morgan's progress in treatment. Based on the author's description, the professional literature, and the latest practice evidence, what occurred to account for their progress or lack of progress?

2. What was the theoretical approach or combination of approaches that the author used with this family?

3. What additional intervention(s) would you recommend for this family? Use the literature and latest evidence to justify your recommendations.

Termination

The Morgans knew that our program helped adoptive families during crises. When the crises subsided, counseling and support services might continue less intensively. Our program usually capped services at one year. After six months, social service adoption monitors had to approve further treatment.

Although Mr. and Mrs. Morgan made progress on their goals, Devon's behavior was slow to change. Based on their progress, the adoption monitor approved treatment services for one full year. However, I provided fewer services during the last six months, mainly because the parents began handling Devon's behavior more effectively during this time.

Devon reached a turning point when his parents refused his driver's license and began enforcing rules around the house. Mr. and Mrs. Morgan finally realized that they could effectively control his behavior by working together, being reasonable, and enforcing consequences that matched the "crime". So often, families give the kids consequences that are unreasonable or impossible to enforce. Devon also began changing after his arrest for breaking and entering. While he did not improve immediately, his attitude slowly changed since that happened.

As we approached termination, I asked Mr. and Mrs. Morgan to make predictions about Devon's future. This intervention often helps parents to prepare for the unexpected and places them in a frame of mind to handle problems in the future. The Morgans predicted that Devon might drop out of school and make life decisions that were less than what they had hoped. However, the Morgans insisted that they would continue loving and supporting him in whatever way they could. He was, after all, their son.

Everyone was ready to terminate. As we met for the last time, the family reviewed their progress. Everyone agreed that Mr. and Mrs. Morgan had succeeded in holding Devon responsible for his behavior. They cited the example of Devon's involvement with Juvenile Court. Mr. and Mrs. Morgan allowed him to suffer the consequences of his actions without serving as a buffer. They also believed that they were better parents for all of their children. Overall, the family terminated happy with their progress.

Follow-Up

I spoke to the Morgans six months after termination. According to Mrs. Morgan, Devon had managed to stay out of trouble. Although he had skipped school on occasion, he was coming home on time and had passed most of his classes. All still seemed well in the Morgan household.

One year after termination, the Morgans completed a follow up questionnaire about their progress. They stated that Devon remained at home, attending school, and the family had required not further services. Mrs. Morgan noted on the form that, "The support service was a life saver for our family, but mainly for me. I will always be grateful."

I heard from the Morgans one last time. They sent me Devon's high school graduation announcement. This was a graduation that I was happy to attend.

Evaluation of Practice

When treatment began, you might remember that I provided the family with several initial Progress Evaluation Scales to complete about their family. Across the board, everyone in the family significantly improved their scores. Devon made the biggest improvement, having his behavior downgraded from severe to moderate. These scales are an excellent way to evaluate practice. The scales allow the family to rate their own behavior over time. Not only do they help practitioners to measure progress, but the family as well. In this case, everyone improved and was happy with the outcome.

Questions

The author presented an interesting, successfully terminated case that involved many issues commonly found in adoption services. Taking a broad view of this case, reevaluate the author's work and your participation through the questions asked throughout the case.

1. Overall, what is your professional opinion of the work performed in this case? As always, refer to the professional literature, practice evidence, your experience, and the experience of student-colleagues when developing your opinion.

2. Based on this review, what additional or alternative approaches could the author have used with this case? That is, if you were the practitioner, how would you have approached this case? Please explain and justify your approach.

3. Were there any specific interventions or strategies that you disliked or liked? Please explain your opinions.

4. What did this case demonstrate that you could use in other practice settings? List the most important things you learned and how you can use these in your practice career.

Bibliography

Aguilera, D. C. (1998). *Crisis intervention: Theory and methodology.* St. Louis: Mosby.
Cline, F. W., & Fay, J. (1992). *Parenting teens with love and logic: Preparing adolescents for responsible adulthood.* New York: Pinon Press.
De Jong, P., & Berg, I. K. (2002). *Interviewing for solutions.* Pacific Grove, CA: Brooks/Cole.
Haley, J. (1987). *Problem-solving therapy.* San Francisco: Jossey-Bass.
Haley, J. (1980). *Leaving home.* New York: McGraw-Hill.
Johnson, J. L. (2004). *Fundamentals of substance abuse practice.* Pacific Grove, CA: Brooks/Cole.
National Association of Social Workers (2000). *The Code of Ethics of the National Association of Social Workers.* Washington, DC: Author.
Turner, F. J. (ed.). (1996). *Social work treatment: Interlocking theoretical approaches* (4th ed.). New York: The Free Press.

4

The Boyds

Steve De Groot

Introduction

Working with couples or families involved in adoption often brings a host of complex and varied issues into the practice equation. International adoption brings with it an additional set of issues and, sometimes, problems. These cases always force practitioners to work with other professionals and agencies including the court system, adoption agencies, as well as various other social service and government agencies. Children involved in international adoption often come from war-torn or impoverished nations. They often hail from the disenfranchised members of their native society. It is necessary to give their culture, race, socioeconomic status, gender, medical history, and ethnicity credence in reference to their presentation and historical records. Professionally, I have found these cases complex, heartbreaking, and the most rewarding.

This case demonstrates many of the aforementioned issues. It centers on a disrupted international adoption. The termination of this adoption involved two starkly contrasting perspectives about the circumstances leading to the court hearing. Family court and Child Protective Services (CPS) held one viewpoint, while the adoptive parents held an entirely different perspective. Family court asked me to bring the two perspectives together so that a just disposition occurred. Caught in the middle of these contrasting opinions were two six-year-old Russian girls and three Chinese girls, all adopted into the same family. As I learned about this case, I understood why the opinions differed. This became a case of misleading information, lies, and inappropriate decision making by otherwise excellent parents.

Alex and Margaret Boyd

A large social service agency referred Alex and Margaret to me for therapy. The referring agent said that the Boyds had recently relinquished their parental rights to two adopted Russian children. The couple voluntarily severed their parental rights after problems developed with their Russian adoption. The court also pressured them because of how Alex and Margaret treated their new daughters. After a CPS investigation, the family court judge presiding over the case gave the Boyds a choice of losing all five of their adopted children or voluntarily relinquishing their parental rights to their two Russian daughters. They opted to relinquish rights to the two girls to save the rest of their family.

Alex and Margaret Enter Therapy

When I first met Alex and Margaret Boyd, they were unhappy to see me. Both Alex and Margaret appeared resistant to the idea that they needed therapy and, more than other court-ordered clients, seemed afraid of the process. As I soon learned, Alex and Margaret had recently endured hurtful and negative contact with social workers from CPS, as well as the two adoption agencies involved in their Russian adoption. Consequently, both Mr. and Mrs. Boyd were reluctant to tell "their story." They entered therapy assuming that I was part of the same adversarial system that they believed had treated them badly.

Mr. Boyd appeared particularly reluctant, even more than his wife did. When we met, I sensed that he was hostile toward the process. In fact, during the first session, I could barely entice him to speak. On the other had, Mrs. Boyd spoke loudly and passionately about their problems, albeit in short and angry words and tones. Given the circumstances of the referral, I could not blame them for being reticent. As I understood their case, the Boyds had just lost their adopted daughters. While they voluntarily severed their own parental rights, family court and CPS forced their hand. I would have to work hard at building a trusting and open relationship with the Boyds. I began by explaining confidentiality and my specific role in the system. I tried to convince Alex and Margaret that I was their ally. At first, they were not "buying" what I was selling.

As stated earlier, the court ordered the Boyds into therapy. When clients are court ordered, practitioners must expect resistance. Furthermore, Mr. Boyd said that the judge chastised both him and his wife, characterizing them as people unwilling to accept responsibility for their actions. The judge was angry that Alex and Margaret blamed their problems on their Russian daughters and the adoption agencies. That is, the "system" believed, according to the judge, that the Boyds blamed their problems on their young daughters. The judge refused to close their case until Alex and Margaret acknowledged their responsibility in this case.

Questions

1. Given what you know about Alex and Margaret and their current situation, what issues would you consider as you prepared to meet them individually for the first time?

2. Since client engagement seemed to be a problem, how would you prepare yourself to overcome the issues the author described?

3. Before reading the next section, think of how you approach involuntary clients in your practice.

Working with Involuntary Clients

Alex and Margaret are what practitioners refer to as "involuntary" clients. They sought help under external duress (Murdach, 1980) after behaving in ways considered troublesome to society (Cingolani, 1984). Their status and presentation differed from so-called voluntary clients who "choose" to seek and, theoretically, accept help (Rooney, 1992). The Boyds hoped to beat a pending court case and have their three daughters returned to their care. In the beginning, the court case compelled the Boyds to attend therapy, but not to make personal changes. Involuntary clients are the source of much disdain in the helping professions because they can be difficult to engage in treatment. Yet, I believe that problems with involuntary clients relate more to the artificial dichotomy (voluntary versus involuntary) than to the person of the client and how they decided to attend therapy.

According to social psychologists Thibaut and Kelley (1959), an involuntary relationship between helper and client contains at least one of the following elements. First, clients must feel forced to remain in the relationship because of physical or legal mandate. Second, they may choose to remain in an involuntary helping relationship because the cost of leaving is too high. Third, clients only believe that they are disadvantaged in the helping relationship because better alternatives are available and they cannot benefit because of the involuntary relationship. Accordingly, Rooney (1992) subdivides involuntary clients into two subgroups: mandated and nonvoluntary clients. According to Rooney (1992), clients are defined as mandated if they "must work with a practitioner as a result of a legal mandate or court order" (pp. 4–5). Nonvoluntary clients enter into a relationship with a helping professional because of "pressure from agencies, other people, and outside events" (p. 5).

Rooney omits an important definition, what constitutes a "voluntary" client. Hence, an important question remains unasked and, therefore, unanswered. I agree with Rooney's (1992) central thesis that most social work education and training focuses on work with so-called voluntary clients, and that little occurs to prepare practitioners for the inevitability of spending much of their professional practice career with clients coerced into treatment by personal issues, persons, agencies, or legal authorities. Social work education and training assumes that most clients are ready, willing, and able to participate in their own treatment (Rooney, 1992). Hence, professional social work education may be out of touch with the real experience of daily practice.

Questions

1. Think back over your educational career. What training or education have you received that specifically prepares you to work with involuntary or coerced clients?

2. What strategies have you learned or practiced that specifically address working with involuntary or coerced clients?

3. What is your attitude about clients involved with the legal system, and what factors contribute to this attitude? Where did this information come from: practice experience, personal bias, instructor bias, or some other place? Do coerced clients deserve the same consideration as other clients, or have they given up their rights because of their "offender" status? Present evidence from the professional literature to defend your position on this issue.

After more than 17 years of practice experience, I have seen few, if any, truly voluntary clients. While there are exceptions (a few people with the time and resources to enter therapy simply to understand their existential place in the world), the vast majority of clients, even in private practice, seek help under coercion. This may be pressure from an outside source such as friends, relatives, or employers or from internal pressures, usually combined with feedback from their environment. Internal coercion usually results from the belief (real or perceived) that people's lives are not going well or that they are not happy or healthy, either individually or in their interpersonal relationships. In other words, rarely have I met a client who, upon awaking in the morning, proclaimed his happiness and then decided to seek therapy! Something or someone forces most people to seek help; a choice they would not otherwise make.

Therefore, it follows that most clients—regardless of practice setting or problems—will resist help, at least initially. Rooney (1992) defines resistance as a constellation of client behaviors that include "provocation, intellectualization, projection, verbosity, seduction, withdrawal, passive compliance, martyrdom, flight from the scene, refusal to answer, lateness for appointments, and changing the subject" (p. 125). With coerced clients, resistance should be expected—considered the normal state of affairs and not an odd circumstance that automatically points to evidence of individual pathology. Yet, in the helping professions, resistance is a pejorative label for clients who oppose what practitioners believe is in their best interest. According to Rooney (1992), "resistance is a label assigned by practitioners to clients who have not acted to the practitioner's satisfaction" (p. 125).

I recommend that practitioners consider client resistance or ambivalence as a normal and expected part of the helping relationship, what Johnson (2004) calls the "dilemma of change" (p. 124). The following passage exemplifies the dilemma of change (Johnson, 2004):

> Consider, if you will, the following definition: a dilemma occurs when a person is presented with two or more options, neither of which appears good. In this light, your client's hesitancy to change is understandable. Clients often say, "My life may be difficult now, but what if I go through all that work to change and my life is still miserable? At least now I'm high and don't worry about life much." This remark is not a function of resistance or denial, but an accurate appraisal of a real possibility. Clients are not eager to change, nor is it certain that they will reap the benefits from achieving sobriety. In fact, many recovering substance abusers have said that it took a significant period of abstinence, sometimes years, before their lives became better. For some, this improvement never happens. People do not change without pain (guilt, shame, embarrassment), struggle (multiple relapses), and/or without considering a permanent return to their previous life ("It wasn't that bad . . . I had some great times on cocaine"). (pp. 124–125)

I intended to approach Alex and Margaret the same as I approach every client, regardless of the circumstances of their referral. I work to develop rapport while seeking to understand my clients in the context of their life, history, issues, and strengths as part of the process of establishing a therapeutic relationship based on mutual trust and agreeable goals (Johnson, 2004). Early on, I do not challenge or confront, but ask questions, listen, and try to understand. Any label (resistant client) that satisfies my need or desire for comfort, ease, or control has no place in the therapeutic context.

Personal History

Alex and Margaret, both 42 years old, had been married 17 years when we met. Alex was a manager in a local manufacturing company and Margaret worked part time for the post office. As practicing Catholics, they always wanted a big family. Alex's parents had eight children and Margaret came from a family of nine. Growing up in large families sometimes makes having a large family unattractive. However, this only made Alex and Margaret want a big family too. Moreover, both said that they always felt "a lot" of pressure to have a big family. Both extended families wanted grandchildren. Since they were the oldest children in their families, it fell to them to be the first to have children.

However, it turned out that Alex was sterile and unable to conceive children. After several years of disappointment and exploring alternatives, the Boyds decided to become adoptive parents. As you will read later, they adopted three daughters from China (currently ages 14, 9, and 6 years old). The Boyds loved kids, and wanted more. This was where their troubles began.

My Background

I am a psychologist and practice in the same city where the Boyds lived. I have been involved in the assessment, evaluation, and treatment of individuals and couples in the child welfare system for more than 17 years. Judges and attorneys frequently referred cases to me for evaluation, and most of my clients were court-ordered. Additionally, I work for a large social service agency through contract from my private practice.

Questions

The therapist brings 17 years of experience working with families and individuals in difficult circumstances surrounding child custody. Assume that you were the therapist assigned this case. Your expertise does not include international adoption or cases involving child custody or abuse.

1. What does the professional literature and Code of Ethics (NASW, 2000) tell you about proceeding with this case?

2. If your agency compelled you to take this case, what steps would you take to prepare yourself to be a competent practitioner for the Boyds?

Engaging Alex and Margaret in Treatment

As stated earlier, the judge ordered Alex and Margaret into individual therapy, insisting that they assume responsibility for the treatment of their children. The judge wanted me to testify that Alex and Margaret articulated the problem and took responsibility for their actions. If successful, this process should allow the Boyds to resolve their legal problems by taking responsibility for their actions in open court. Please understand that I was asked to perform a specific therapeutic function in this case. I was to help them take responsibility. Hence, in many ways, the court enlisted me as their ally in helping resolve this case. This fact presented a tremendous barrier between the Boyds and me, one that we would have to overcome for therapy to succeed. I wanted the Boyds to have their children back, and so did the judge. My job was to point them toward the solution.

From court documents, I learned that the Boyd's two Russian daughters were diagnosed with Reactive Attachment Disorder and Fetal Alcohol Syndrome (FAS). Fetal Alcohol Syndrome is comprised of a set of disorders resulting from the mother's alcohol consumption while the fetus was in utero, a common occurrence in Russia. The symptoms of this disorder often present as physical, mental, and neurobehavioral in nature. Individuals born with FAS often present with low birth weight and frequently exhibit difficulties in judgment, learning, and behavior problems.

Mr. and Mrs. Boyd knew that the judge expected them to admit blame and accept responsibility for the problems in their family. Yet, they did not believe they were responsible. Hence, the judge's request exacerbated their anxiety. They entered treatment defensively, with a high degree of suspicion about the intent of the therapeutic process.

First Meetings

The judge ordered Alex and Margaret into individual therapy. They were not allowed to meet as a couple as part of their court-ordered treatment. Therefore, I met with the Boyds on the same day, one hour apart. As we began meeting, Alex and Margaret told almost the exact same stories. From how they described the problems to who they believed was to blame, Alex and Margaret's account of their problems were identical. My progress notes read as if I was working only one case. Either they rehearsed their stories well, or they were telling the truth. I had to find out. At this stage, neither would acknowledge their role and responsibility for how they treated their adopted daughters from Russia.

I tried to engage them by providing a safe place for Alex and Margaret to vent their frustrations, how they felt misled by the local adoption agency, and how the system did not believe their stories. Both Alex and Margaret said they were frustrated, hopeless, and confused. Furthermore, Alex and Margaret felt unequipped to handle the girls once they identified the girls' behavioral problems. Eventually, both Alex and Margaret made statements such as, "I was ill-equipped to deal with the problems these girls presented."

It was important that Mr. and Mrs. Boyd saw me as an ally in their lives. Up to now, Alex and Margaret believed that every person involved in their case placed the full blame on them for their problems with their adopted daughters. I tried to give them a sense of an alliance. As we worked to build our relationship, I identified two important issues to help with engagement. First, Alex and Margaret needed someone to "hear" their sense of betrayal by the adoption agency and CPS. In fact, the Boyds were indeed misled and given misinformation about the girls they thought they were adopting from Russia (see below). They were lied to every step of the way. I acknowledged that they were misled, and that this placed them in a position of having daughters with serious troubles to care for. I also acknowledged that they had every right to feel betrayed. With the seriousness of the girls' problems, there was no way they would successfully adjust to the Boyds family situation.

My acknowledgment of the betrayal seemed to provide the Boyds some emotional reprieve. They were no longer the sole bearers of responsibility for the problems that had occurred in this adoption. It was important for them to have someone in a professional role believe them. I spent several sessions listening to Alex and Margaret talk about their feelings regarding the adoption. However, I also felt the need to help Alex and Margaret identify areas where they mishandled the information and made bad decisions that contributed to the eventual problems with CPS and the court system.

As stated above, it is important for clients to believe they have an ally in therapy, especially when they face legal problems. Helping clients assume responsibility for their actions does not preclude being their ally. For therapy to be successful, practitioners must develop a rapport with clients before work proceeds. Only after clients feel safe can they acknowledge their mistakes and/or wrongdoings. I allowed the Boyds to spend several sessions voicing their anger, frustration, and resentment toward the adoption agency that misled them. Once voiced, it became appropriate to guide the Boyds in the direction toward self-responsibility.

Questions

1. How do you handle hostile clients that refuse to speak? How about clients who speak angrily and fast-paced? Please explain yourself.

2. Before moving ahead with the case, consider the issues involved with client rapport and engagement. What is your approach to this issue, and to what importance do you give professional relationship building?

3. What are the most important factors in client engagement?

4. What percentage of your time do you spend working on and/or practicing your engagement skills? List several ways that you can improve or practice engagement skills.

However, before we could redirect their anger, I had to understand their story. Below, I describe the circumstances that led the Boyds into court, and eventually into my office as court-ordered clients.

The Boyds' Drama Begins

Initially, Alex and Margaret Boyd wanted to adopt two children from Russia. They were already adoptive parents to three daughters from China when they entered the latest adoption process. They adopted their first daughter from China ten years earlier. They subsequently adopted two additional daughters from the same orphanage in China five and two years earlier. By all accounts, Alex and Margaret were exemplary adoptive parents, admired by everyone in local and international adoption circles.

Their First Adoptions

When the Boyds adopted their children from China, they used a local adoption agency that held a contract with an adoption agency in China. The local agency completed the Boyds' home study. When the agency approved their application, the local agency contacted the Chinese agency and made the appropriate arrangements to identify children for adoption. Once identified, the Boyds flew to China to meet with officials of the Chinese adoption agency.

The Boyds remained in China for two weeks while the government completed their paperwork. During the two weeks, Alex and Margaret met and spent significant time with their new daughter. Mr. Boyd remembered that he "fell in love" with her immediately. He knew that she was his daughter the minute he held her in his arms. Finally, Alex and Margaret had a family. Mrs. Boyd expressed the same emotions when she described the first time she met their daughter. The second and third adoption from China went as smoothly as the first. There were no delays and within two weeks, they were back on an airplane to the United States. In all, Alex and Margaret were the proud adoptive parents of three girls.

The Boyd's adoption experiences in China were positive and productive. From all accounts, the three children adapted successfully by making the appropriate adjustments to life in the United States. The Boyds were doting parents. They spent hours researching cultural issues and differences and made every effort to allow their daughters to understand and embrace their Chinese heritage. They became public spokespersons about the benefits of international adoption. They established healthy and strong relationships with their adoption agency. Despite the significant cost of adoption, the Boyds received support to make their dreams a reality. Mr. Boyd's job with a local manufacturing company provided significant support to their adoption process. His employer contributed $5000 for each child's adoption and provided leave time for Mr. Boyd without negatively affecting his job rating or status.

After adopting their third child from China, and in cooperation with the adoption agency, Mr. and Mrs. Boyd helped start an international adoption support group. Frequently, they arranged to meet and engage in supportive activities with other couples that utilized the services of international adoption. Alex and Margaret became the model of successful international adoption.

Pursuing Russian Adoption

When their first three children became older (approximately fourteen, nine, and six years old), Alex and Margaret considered international adoption again. They wanted to share their loving family environment with more children in need. This time, they wanted to adopt children from Russia. They watched a television show that investigated orphanages in Russia and were appalled by the horrible living conditions there. They located information about adopting children from Russia out of concern.

As the television show demonstrated, the fall of communism precipitated an increased need for adoptive parents in a nation with a growing orphan population. However, their previous adoption agency did not work in Russia. A different local adoption agency obtained a contract with the Russian government to oversee all Russian international adoptions in this area. Staff at their original agency encouraged Mr. and Mrs. Boyd to work with the other adoption agency to pursue information about adopting Russian children.

Alex and Margaret's adoption history and reputation in the international adoption community impressed the new agency. Because of their previous international adoption experiences, the agency encouraged the Boyds to pursue their dream of adopting children from Russia. The agency also informed them that Russian rules and regulations regarding adoption were strict. They required the Boyds to pass a series of psychological evaluations and other assessment tools. This differed from their Chinese experiences. The Boyds passed with "flying colors." They were excellent candidates for adoption.

Happily, the Boyds noted that their new adoption agency seemed particularly interested in facilitating successful adoptions. After their approval as adoptive parents, the agency provided Alex and Margaret with profiles of several Russian children. They noticed that many of the profiles described the children positively, claiming that the children had no problems to worry about. From these profiles, Mr. and Mrs. Boyd found two girls that interested them. The profiles described these girls as well adjusted, warm, friendly, well behaved, and pleasant children. The profiles also said that both girls were six years old. However, the Boyds noticed that both girls looked much younger in their pictures.

Adoptive parents often worry about how small Russian children seem. That is, Russian children are often considerably smaller than North American children are. A majority of children from Russian orphanages fall below the fifth percentile in height and weight. Failure to thrive is usually evident within the first six months of life, and the pattern continues. Failure to thrive can come from poor nutrition or complications of a variety of causes, including Fetal Alcohol Syndrome (FAS). At the time of the adoption proceeding, nobody explored the cause of the girls' markedly small stature. The profiles also failed to discuss the circumstances that led to the girls becoming candidates for adoption. There was no mention of their mothers. However, since they had no obvious problems, the Boyds did not worry.

Questions

Based on the information provided so far, please respond to the following questions about this case.

1. What is your first hunch regarding the adoption? Explore the practice literature about international adoption to examine issues surrounding Russian adoption. If the literature does not speak specifically about this, are there other countries with similar issues that are relevant to this discussion?

2. If you were the adoption worker in this case, what is your next direction of inquiry and assessment? What would you advise the Boyds at this point? What information would you need to collect to perform a comprehensive and/or multi-systemic assessment? (See Chapter 1).

3. Examine the literature to learn the causes of the children's small stature and failure to thrive. What factors contribute to the issues and what do they suggest for adoptive parents?

Travel to Russia

Eventually, Mr. and Mrs. Boyd arranged a trip to Russia to adopt their new daughters. This trip lasted ten days. During that time, Mr. and Mrs. Boyd were to make a final decision about whether to complete the adoptions from the Russian orphanage. The Boyds flew to Moscow with the intent of adopting the two girls they had been encouraged to consider. Mr. and Mrs. Boyd noted the great amount of attention focused on them and their qualifications to adopt children from Russia. Alex and Margaret spent most of their time with bureaucrats and in meetings. They did not have sufficient opportunities to meet and get to know their prospective daughters. In hindsight, Alex and Margaret wondered if the Russian authorities kept them away from the girls on purpose. Approximately five days into their visit, Alex and Margaret had only one brief opportunity to meet with the girls.

At one point, the Russian government tried to deny Mr. and Mrs. Boyd's application for adoption. They discovered that Mr. Boyd developed epilepsy as a teenager, raising questions about his ability to adopt the children. The Boyds scrambled to obtain medical documents indicating that Alex had not experienced epileptic symptoms in more than 20 years. At that time, Alex began taking medication to control his symptoms. Once the authorities had medical proof of his health status, the adoption process continued.

Finally, on the day before they were to leave, the Boyds spent time with the girls they wanted to adopt. The agency granted them an opportunity to have both girls on an overnight visit, with the intent of giving Alex and Margaret the chance to "get to know" their prospective children. Mr. and Mrs. Boyd noted that the children seemed distant during the visit. They defined the girls' behavior as "unruly." According to the Boyds, the girls seemed unwilling to express or accept affection. Moreover, the Boyds later stated that both girls said that they "wanted" to stay in Russia rather than live with the Boyds. Alex and Margaret shared their concerns with the Russian professionals. All of the material they had seen claimed that the girls were well behaved and well adjusted. The girls that Alex and Margaret met did not match their profile. They became worried that the Russian agency was not telling them the truth.

However, their emotions won. That is, Alex and Margaret decided to adopt the girls despite their bad experience and the girls' apparent resistance to becoming adopted. Alex and Margaret decided that the girls' resistance was in response to the significant adjustment process they were about to experience. They recalled that their Chinese daughters said the same things before they were adopted. Consequently, the Boyds—and the adoption officials in Russia—minimized the severity of the children's behavior during the overnight visit. At the end of their ten-day stay in Moscow, Alex and Margaret signed official papers certifying the adoption of the two girls. Mr. and Mrs. Boyd happily returned to the United States with the two girls in their custody, ready to integrate them into their already diverse family.

The New Family Returns Home to Problems

The Boyds told me that the girls had immediate problems adjusting to their new home. They continued being unemotional and distant. Alex and Margaret commented that they wondered if they actually adopted the two girls they had originally chosen. The profiles described those girls as warm, friendly, and pleasant. Mr. and Mrs. Boyd characterized their girls as unruly, cold, and resistant. The girls remained resistant to any attempts the Boyd family made toward emotional bonding. Alex and Margaret described the two girls as unwilling to allow either parent to touch them. The girls took steps to avoid being near the Boyds, remaining in separate rooms whenever possible. Alex and Margaret added that the girls seemed resentful about any parental directive or instruction given to them.

As their troubles and doubts mounted, Alex and Margaret made monthly reports to the adoption agency. The reports detailed their progress with the adoption experience. The Boyds used these reports to explain their problems. They characterized the adoption experience negatively. The children resisted acclimating themselves to the family and refused parental direction. Alex and Margaret claimed that both girls appeared defiant, resistant, and controlling.

One of their daughters developed serious problems with food. Alex and Margaret said that she either "gorged" herself to the point of sickness or refused to eat entirely. Typically, her behavior was contrary to her requests. For example, Margaret described situations where she made a large meal, giving each child large servings because they said they were hungry. Once the food was prepared, the girl refused to eat or even sit at the table with the family. Consequently, Alex and Margaret began allowing her to skip family meals. The Boyds also discovered that their daughter sneaked food. On one occasion, she reportedly snuck into the kitchen and ate a box of pastries while everyone else slept. From this point forward, food became a central issue in the Boyd household.

Alex and Margaret claimed that they could not bond with either daughter. They frequently addressed these issues with the adoption agency. However, the Boyds believed that the adoption agency minimized their problems. The agency characterized the problems as normal adjustment issues that all children experience in that situation. They also discovered that the local agency did not forward their actual report to the Russian government. The caseworker collected the reports and wrote a summary, leaving out the problems and highlighting the success. The Russian government only knew what the caseworker summaries told them. Therefore, they had no idea that the adoption was troubled.

As time passed, Alex and Margaret believed that they were caught in a "double bind" scenario. Their international adoption support group looked to the Boyds as leaders and models for international adoption. However, they were having significant problems with this adoption and the difficulties ran contrary to this perception. Consequently, Alex and Margaret chose not to discuss their problems with their friends and colleagues. Unfortunately, the problems became worse. The Boyds claimed that the girls resisted any parental influence. They reported numerous instances where the girls reacted with oppositional and defiant behavior when the Boyds attempted to exert parental guidance and instruction. The girls began destroying their rooms, breaking toys and furniture, and trying to beat their other daughters in fits of rage. At one point, Margaret described the girls' behavior similar to someone "possessed by demons." The girls would go from calm to hostile and destructive behavior in a "second."

Questions

The Boyds repeatedly described the girls' behavior as unruly and defiant. They characterized the children as unwilling or unable to show or receive affection from their new parents. The children went to great lengths to avoid being in close proximity with their new parents. Given these observations, respond to the following questions.

1. What are you thinking about regarding this case? Specifically, what problems do you suspect?

2. With the limited information provided, consider Mr. and Mrs. Boyd from the strengths perspective. Please take this time to make an inventory of the Boyd's strengths as well as the strengths of various systems the Boyd's encountered.

3. Prepare an initial assessment of the girls. What additional information would you need to complete a multi-axial DSM-IV-TR diagnosis? What steps would you take to acquire this information?

4. Mr. and Mrs. Boyd's history with international adoption was stellar. Their three daughters from China were thriving under their care. Consider the respect afforded the Boyds within their systems. What complications would their reputation cause in this case? As their therapist, how would you address these concerns?

Finding Help for Their Daughters

Alex and Margaret eventually sought counsel from a psychiatrist at a local university. The psychiatrist did not meet either of the adopted girls. However, after speaking with the Boyds, she offered a preliminary diagnosis. She told the Boyds that the information they provided led her to characterize the girls as exhibiting symptoms of Reactive Attachment Disorder (APA, 2000).

Reactive Attachment Disorder presents with a markedly disjointed or inappropriate social attachment, often caused by a lack of parental bonding in infancy. Symptoms of this disorder usually occur before five years of age. According to the DSM-IV-TR (APA, 2000), Reactive Attachment Disorder is characterized by inhibitions or disinhibitions of behavior. Clients who present with inhibited behavior exhibit social responsiveness in an excessively inhibited, hyper-vigilant, or contrary manner. Clients that fall within the confines of disinhibitions fail to be selective in their attachments. These children exert the same attachment to strangers as to primary caregivers. The behaviors as described by the Boyds met the criteria of Reactive Attachment Disorder, with inhibitions (APA, 2000).

Mistaken Judgment

Unfortunately, after receiving this preliminary diagnosis of the symptoms, the Boyds did not seek further help for their adopted daughters. The Boyds allowed their pride and community reputation to win. They refused professional help because they did not want their colleagues and the original adoption agency to know that they were failing.

In the absence of treatment, the situation deteriorated. Eventually, Alex and Margaret resorted to imposing rigid and concrete rules on their daughters. The Boyds believed that the girls had simple behavioral problems that required discipline. The girls were mentally ill and unable to respond appropriately. However, the Boyds failed to understand the psychiatrist and treated the girls as if they were misbehaving. They decided the time had come to exert firm parental guidance and set limits and boundaries.

Alex and Margaret began their new disciplinary approach by limiting the girls' access to food. They forced the girls to eat only what Margaret offered. If the girls refused a meal, they went without food. Sometimes, the girls would not eat for several days at a time. Alex and Margaret believed that they would get hungry and eat "sooner or later." Alex and Margaret never seemed to notice that the girls were not eating and losing weight.

The Boyds also decided to remove the girls from school and other social situations. They essentially isolated the girls from everyone, hoping that their extreme form of "grounding" would "snap" the girls out of their misbehavior. As a result, Alex and Margaret kept the girls in the house under their watchful eye, twenty-four hours per day and seven days a week. Everyone became prisoners in the house: the girls and the Boyds. For weeks, nobody had a reprieve from this restrictive and negative environment.

Enter the Adoption Agency

Eventually, the caseworker from the adoption agency came to their home for a visit. She wanted to meet with the two girls to perform a personal assessment of their progress. The caseworker was appalled when she heard about the Boyds' new rules.

Alex and Margaret denied the caseworker access to the girls during the unannounced home visit. Furthermore, they accused the caseworker's adoption agency of being deceitful in providing and omitting information regarding the girls. Because of the deception, they wanted no further contact with this particular adoption agency. The Boyds essentially kicked the caseworker out of their house.

Although different types of adoption have different policies and procedures, there are minimal standards about agency involvement in any adoption. When a child is adopted, the caseworker should have minimal contact to assess the child's progress in the adjustment and attachment process. Each state establishes minimum criteria for contacts with the adoptive families. In this particular case, the caseworker received monthly reports, but had had no personal contact with the children in six months. It is reasonable to believe that the caseworker "should have" known what was going on and visited more often. However, Alex and Margaret did not have the right to bar the caseworker from seeing the children.

Questions

Imagine yourself as the caseworker, wanting to see the Russian girls that you are legally responsible for through your agency. When you arrived at the house, the adoptive parents refused access to the girls.

1. Explore your local or state laws regarding the rights of adoptive parents and agencies within six months of a legal adoption. According to these laws and policies, what rights do you have as the caseworker?

2. Based on your findings in question 1, what recourse do you have in this instance? Please explain your ideas and proposed actions.

Enter CPS

With access to the children denied, the caseworker immediately contacted Children's Protective Services (CPS). Within hours, CPS was at Alex and Margaret's door, demanding access to the girls. The CPS worker, accompanied by two police officers, required the Boyds to allow them to see the Russian girls. Upon entering the home, the caseworker discovered that both of the girls were emaciated. They looked as if they suffered from malnutrition. Furthermore, both girls presented with significant bruising all over their bodies. Their frail condition led the CPS worker to call an ambulance to take the girls immediately to a local hospital.

Court Proceedings Begin

This is how Alex and Margaret Boyd entered the child welfare system. Because of the poor condition of the girls, they became involved at family and criminal court. CPS removed their three remaining daughters the following day. When the case came to my attention, all of their adopted children were in a foster home. None of the children was allowed contact with Mr. or Mrs. Boyd. The Boyds attended an emergency hearing at the family court with a referee. The referee decided to keep all five daughters in foster care. Criminal court also charged Alex and Margaret with child abuse.

After their initial hearing with the referee, Alex and Margaret's case landed with a local judge in the family court division. At the first court hearing, Mr. and Mrs. Boyd were represented by an attorney. Their attorney advised them that if they had hope of regaining custody of their daughters from China, they would need to relinquish their parental rights to their daughters from Russia. The Boyds were out of viable options. They reluctantly relinquished their parental rights to their adopted Russian daughters at the hearing. Alex and Margaret pleaded guilty to a reduced charge of domestic violence and were sentenced to probation and charged fines. The courts also referred Alex and Margaret to me for individual counseling. The judge made the order specific. Both parents were to participate in individual counseling. The court disallowed couples or family therapy at this time.

Questions

Alex and Margaret found themselves in a difficult situation. Either they were terrific and caring parents victimized by a corrupt international adoption system, or they were abusive parents, incapable of handling two difficult girls from Russia. Either way, Alex and Margaret made a bad situation worse with the choices they made regarding the care of their Russian daughters. Assume that you are the therapist assigned to treat the Boyds, and respond to the following questions.

1. Explore the international adoption literature to determine the relevant laws and policies pertaining to international adoption. What agencies have significant roles in the process in your state?

2. What steps would you take to determine the truth of this case? How would you determine whether the Boyds were fit parents victimized by a bad system, or unfit parents that made bad decisions?

Now that the author has presented Alex and Margaret's personal histories and before reading further, perform the following exercises based on your education, experience, the professional literature, and best practice evidence. To increase the learning potential of this exercise, you may want to do this in a small group with other students.

3. Based on the information contained above, construct a three-generation genogram and eco-map that represent Alex and Margaret's personal, familial, and environmental circumstances. What further information do you need to

complete this exercise? What patterns do these two important graphical assessment tools demonstrate?

4. Develop a list of Alex and Margaret's problems and strengths.

5. Write a three-page narrative assessment that encompasses Alex and Margaret's multi-systemic issues and strengths. Review Chapter 1, if needed. This narrative should provide a comprehensive and multi-systemic explanation of their life as they undergo therapy with the author.

6. Try to identify the theoretical model or approach that you used to guide your assessment. According to the literature, what other theoretical options are available and how would these change the nature of your assessment?

7. End by developing multi-axial DSM-IV-TR diagnoses for both Alex and Margaret. Be sure to look for evidence of multiple diagnoses on Axis I. Provide the list of client symptoms that you used to justify your diagnostic decisions. What, if any, information was missing that would make this an easier task?

8. Based on your determination, plan your approach for treatment. What initial goals would you have in treatment with the Boyds? What steps would you take to ensure that your treatment addressed the needs of the court, the girls, and the Boyd family?

Alex and Margaret's Therapy Continues

As time passed, I slowly moved the focus of therapy from allowing Alex and Margaret the chance to vent to identifying their mistakes and responsibilities, including their failure to seek professional help for the girls after the psychiatrist diagnosed their problems. As our relationship developed, Alex and Margaret overcame their initial defensiveness and discussed their conflicts. They admitted to not seeking out services and identifying problems when they occurred. Each claimed that they felt pressured to handle their problems alone, because of their reputation in the local international adoption circles. In essence, the Boyds allowed their pride to get in the way of taking appropriate action.

Eventually the Boyds said that they were "ill-equipped" to deal with the problems the girls presented. They came to believe and accept that they mishandled the girls from the onset. While Alex began as the most resistant, he ultimately became the first to acknowledge his role and responsibility in their problems with the girls. Margaret remained defensive and angry longer into treatment. Both Alex and Margaret rightly maintained that they were misled, and that was not their fault. However, they also acknowledged that they did not take appropriate action when it counted on behalf of the girls.

My Theoretical Approach

I used two general tactics with the Boyds. As part of forming a therapeutic relationship, I allowed the Boyds to vent their feelings. Initially, Alex and Margaret expressed their feelings and emotions of turmoil, angst, and frustration regarding their failed attempts to improve the behavior of their daughters. Secondly, I used a more direct approach designed to help Alex and Margaret move from blaming the system and girls to taking responsibility for their actions, as the judge requested.

I primarily used a cognitive-behavioral approach (Payne, 1997; Turner, 1996) with the Boyds. Typically, in cognitive-behavioral therapy, therapist and clients identify inaccurate cognitions. Once identified, client and therapist work together to change these erroneous thoughts. Cognitive-behavioral therapy posits that changing erroneous thoughts ultimately leads to changes in behavior. It was evident that Alex and Margaret have both held a negative cognitive frame of reference about their daughters and the adoption system. They believed that the girls were purposefully behaving in oppositional and defiant ways and that the system was out to get them.

The Boyds did not consider the possibility that the girls were behaving self-protectively, keeping emotional distance between themselves and others to prevent further loss, pain, and grief. They also did not consider that parental bonding might have been impossible for the girls, given their early childhood experiences in Russia, most likely never having the opportunity to bond with their mothers immediately after their birth. Instead, Alex and Margaret believed that they could change their daughters' behavior through discipline (Turner, 1996).

To fully understand and accept their responsibility, Alex and Margaret had to change their thoughts about their daughters and the reasons for their behavior. This change involved Alex and Margaret identifying their inappropriate responses to their daughters' behavior, rather than blaming their recently adopted daughters for their behavior (Payne, 1997).

I was also interested in exploring the Boyd family dynamics. I thought it would be helpful to explore relationships within the family through a visual interpretation. Hence, I created an eco-map and genogram with both clients. An eco-map and genogram symbolizes a family as they relate to each other and outside systems that interact with the family. Eco-maps use universal symbols to determine the relationship and the energy projected within the systems under study.

These exercises successfully provided a visual aid for additional discussion. It also served as an effective tool in characterizing different individuals within their system as they related to each other. To maximize the effectiveness of the exercises, it must remain a fluid and active part of therapy. We continued to utilize the eco-map and made modifications as required throughout the therapeutic process. As part of the termination process, we contrasted their original eco-map with a new one completed during the final session.

Major Intervention

I wanted the Boyds to incorporate an active exercise in their treatment, designed to precipitate changes in their thought processes and allow them to act on their changes in a productive manner. This exercise involved Alex and Margaret independently writing letters of apology to the Russian girls. In similar cases, I have found this intervention a powerful tool, one that moves clients to greater depth in treatment. As the Boyds became willing to acknowledge their responsibility, I believed that writing apology letters might take them the rest of the way toward the court's goal.

To be effective, the letters needed to express their role in and responsibility for what CPS called child abuse. However, before this intervention could work, Alex and Margaret needed to acknowledge their responsibility and bad decisions forthrightly. For example, they needed to identify their inappropriate response to the girls' food problems. Their refusal to feed the girls resulted in malnutrition that led to the bruising. Apparently, malnutrition caused the girls' bruises, not physical abuse. The Boyds should have fed their daughters and sought professional help for the problems.

Question

In this instance, the therapist chose a letter-writing exercise to address his client's cognitive distortions. What other therapeutic means are available to precipitate an acknowledgment of cognitive error and effectively motivate change?

The Boyds worked on their letters for several weeks. Initially, they resisted this assignment, especially the part about accepting responsibility. Alex and Margaret feared that the courts would use their letters against them. I explained that their court-ordered therapy was supposed to show evidence of taking responsibility. In fact, the letters were exactly what the judge wanted to resolve the case.

Eventually the Boyds began writing their letters. They brought their letters to therapy each week. We read and discussed them, and I offered suggestions about how they could improve. I returned the letters at the end of each session, suggesting that they lessen their focus on the girls' behavior and increase their focus on their responsibilities. Eventually, the Boyds complied. The letters of apology served as an effective tool to walk Alex and Margaret through the cognitive changes needed to accept responsibility.

Interestingly, Mr. Boyd appeared to somewhat surpass his wife in acknowledging his previous lack of responsibility. He attributed his inappropriate responses to his lack of education, personal frustration, and insecurities. Mrs. Boyd continued to resist. She experienced difficulty acknowledging the mistakes she made in dealing with the girls' problems. The following is Mrs. Boyd's letter of apology. The difference in tone between the two letters is noteworthy.

> Dear Ivana and Svetlana,
>
> I hope that you are doing well in your new home. Sadly, it was impossible for you to remain with us. Looking back on our trip to Russia, we anticipated the addition of two new girls to our family. We had a lot of love to give you, but knew little about you. We hoped that fulfillment in relationship would be yours. This will take a great deal of work, especially on your part, so please be patient. It may be scary in the beginning. However, in the end, there can be healing. As always, we wish for you the best in life.
>
> There may be questions in your minds that are too complex to answer. We don't have a simple or single explanation for why things didn't work out. If only we had been prepared for some specific techniques to help you . . . if only we could have looked beyond the behaviors to the actual issues . . . but all the "if onlys" cannot change reality. Therefore, we learn from it and have moved ahead with greater wisdom. If you remember, I had talked to you about being victorious, and that you could "win over your past hurts" and then there would be opportunities for you to help others to be "over-comers" someday.
>
> I believe that you can get to that finish line! Sometimes the race we run goes uphill a lot, so you have to work extra hard to get to the top. If you fall, there will be someone to pick you up and encourage you. Alex and I understand we could not have helped you by ourselves. We were struggling and we did not fully realize the hurdles in front of us. We tried running alone, but it wasn't enough to help you. We wish we had sought professional advice while you were living here. Therefore, now it's very important that you rely on the expertise of others. It requires a team effort to win your marathon. We are cheering for you and hope you will be successful adults.
>
> We regret that we cannot be your "forever family." You were innocent, helpless babies born in Russia to a young, teenage mother who was still growing up. Infants demand a lot of sacrifice from their caregivers as they have so many needs. Unfortunately, your birth parents also had many unmet needs of their own, as well as some serious personal problems. Sadly, that made it impossible for them to nurture you.
>
> Later, you felt alone and perhaps unwanted because you had to live in two orphanages. Were you angry or hurt? Maybe when we came to get you, you hoped for your birth parents instead, and then we whisked you far away to America. Now, you would finally have everything you wanted, whenever you wanted it. You could escape your bad memories. You were going on a vacation. However, we wanted to blend you into our family. Maybe you feel we let you down, and in some ways, maybe we did.
>
> Remember, these circumstances were beyond your control. You did not ask to be born in Russia, you may not have even wanted to come to America, or understand what "family" really meant. We apologize for adding to the string of disasters in your lives. We failed you and hope you will be able to forgive us. Grab onto your future by releasing yourself from the blames. Someday you will be able to rise up on the wings of eagles.
>
> Sincerely, Mrs. Boyd

This letter focuses predominantly on the girls. It discusses the struggles the girls went through. It does not identify the role Margaret played in the girls' abuse.

Based on this letter, I believed that Margaret needed to continue in therapy until she understood and accepted her role and responsibility in the girls' abuse.

In contrast, Mr. Boyd seemed to grasp his role and responsibility. This fact alone would have necessitated that Mr. and Mrs. Boyd continue in individual, rather than conjoint counseling. The differing levels at which they progressed through therapy would have made conjoint counseling ineffective. The letters addressed the girls from a significantly different frame of reference. Mrs. Boyd's letter wished the girls well in their new home. The tone of the letter appeared to indicate that the girls' behavior prevented them from remaining with the family. Her second sentence demonstrated this point well, when Margaret said, "Sadly, it wasn't possible for *you* to remain with us." This statement contrasts dramatically with Mr. Boyd's beginning sentence.

> Dear Ivana and Svetlana,
>
> I wish to express to you my deep sadness in the way I treated both of you. My discipline with both of you did not work, and I believe that I hurt your feelings and developmental progress in becoming a whole person. I can express my sorrow and deep down feeling in how I thought it was the right thing to do. I am truly sorry and regretful in these areas.
>
> My frustrations with both of you were something that I was not ready to handle at the time. I gave you many chances to communicate and tell me your sides of the story and maybe you couldn't. I separated you apart from the rest of the family and this was wrong in not working harder at including you in our family. My insensitive emotions to your needs probably caused you to pull apart even more from me and the rest of the family. I guess what I want you girls to know above all else, is that it is not your fault.
>
> Your biological parents did not know how to raise and develop you properly enough before you were born, as well as afterward. It wasn't your fault when you came into our lives, because of my methods and processes of what I tried to do for you and what I thought would help. I was not equipped to do this right, and I am again very sorry for all that you had to go through in your lives when you resided with us. Therefore, in the end of this letter, I wish you to know that you have a new beginning. God has made you for a special purpose and I ask that you continue to seek it. You are not an accident, but are beautiful people who hopefully can find fulfillment and contentment in this world. I pray with all my heart that you seek God's will, find it, and pursue it with all your abilities.
>
> God bless you, Ivana and Svetlana.
>
> With all my love and prayers,
>
> Mr. Boyd

Termination

In the end, I presented these letters to the court as part of Alex and Margaret's termination process with the child welfare system. We determined that the experience was traumatic and disadvantageous to everyone. The court believed the Boyds had demonstrated significant growth in their knowledge of the importance to reach out and receive help in times of difficulty. The court also restored their three daughters to their care. At last contact, both Mr. and Mrs. Boyd were again involved in an adoptive parent support group. They were reaching out to make use of appropriate community services, particularly those available through their church.

Questions

After completing the court-ordered therapy session, the judge agreed to reinstitute custody of the Boyd's three older children from China. These children spent two months in foster care, while the case proceeded through the court system.

1. Explore the professional literature to determine how the court-imposed separation would affect this family.

2. Based on your findings, what recommendations or services would you present to the Boyd family to aid in the reunification process?

I met with the Boyds for twelve individual sessions in addition to one joint session as part of the termination process. At the completion of our work together, they demonstrated to the court that they were capable of taking responsibility for their actions. The judge, satisfied with their progress, closed the case.

Questions

The author presented an interesting case. Taking a broad view of this case, reevaluate the author's work by responding to the following questions.

1. Take a moment to review Alex and Margaret's progress. Based on the author's description, the professional literature, and the latest practice evidence, what occurred to account for their progress?

2. What was the theoretical approach or combination of approaches that appeared to work best?

3. Based on the work you have done earlier, what additional intervention(s) would you recommend? Use the literature and latest evidence to justify your recommendations.

4. Overall, what is your professional opinion of the work performed in this case? As always, refer to the professional literature, practice evidence, your experience, and the experience of student-colleagues when developing your opinion.

5. Based on this review, what additional or alternative approaches could have been used with this case? That is, if you were the practitioner, how would you have approached this case? Please explain and justify your approach.

6. As part of the termination process, what concerns would you express to Mr. and Mrs. Boyd about the long-term effects of the process they have been through? What supports could you offer?

7. Describe the benefits and challenges of using individual therapy with Mr. and Mrs. Boyd. The therapist recommended continued individual therapy. As a therapist, would you work toward conjoint therapy/couples therapy, or continue with individual therapy for the Boyds? What brings you to this conclusion?

8. The author had one role, to help the Boyds accept responsibility for their actions. Hence, review the code of ethics and practice literature. Did the Boyds have the right to self-determination in this therapy? Moreover, did the author handle this case in a way that involved the Boyds in developing their own treatment? If not, how can this work be squared with the code of ethics? Is the context of this case different from court-ordered clients that have other problems, such as substance abuse? Explain your position on these issues.

9. What did this case demonstrate that you could use in other practice settings? List the most important things you learned by studying this case and how you could use them in your practice career.

Bibliography

American Psychiatric Association (2000). *Diagnostic and statistical manual of mental disorders* (4th ed., TR). Washington, DC: Author.

Cingolani, J. (1984). Social conflict perspective on work with involuntary clients. *Social Work, 29:* 442–446.

Johnson, J. L. (2004). *Fundamentals of substance abuse practice.* Pacific Grove, CA: Brooks/Cole.

Murdach, A. D. (1980). Bargaining and persuasion with non-voluntary clients. *Social Work, 25*(6): 458.

National Association of Social Workers (2000). *Code of Ethics of the National Association of Social Workers.* Washington, DC: Author.

Payne, M. (1997). *Modern social work theory* (2nd ed.). Chicago, IL: Lyceum Books, Inc.

Rooney, R. H. (1992). *Strategies for working with involuntary clients.* New York: Columbia University Press.

Thibaut, J. W., & Kelley, H. H. (1959). *The social psychology of groups.* New York: Wiley.

Turner, F. J. (ed.). (1996). *Social work treatment: Interlocking theoretical approaches* (4th ed.). New York: The Free Press.

Travis

Robin L. Smith

Introduction

Child Protective Services (CPS) removed Travis from his biological parents and placed him in foster care until he was adopted by a single-parent female. Travis's case looks at what happened in his life that led to his adoption. However, my main reason for writing this case was to examine the therapeutic "lens" used to address the child's struggles with adoption. The case also evaluates whether the approach I chose was appropriate for Travis's case by looking at its strengths and weaknesses.

Travis's History

Travis was a thirteen-year-old African American male in counseling because of fighting with his peers, suicidal thoughts, depression, and poor social skills. He was living in a single-parent, female, African American home. Ms. Debra Wright adopted Travis when he was twelve years old. Originally, Travis was the only child of Shirley and Raymond Evans. Travis both witnessed and experienced abuse, neglect, and domestic violence in his parents' home. According to CPS workers, Travis was beaten, starved, and emotionally abused. CPS removed Travis from the Evans home and, eventually, Ms. Wright adopted him.

Adoption Worker

I was the adoption specialist assigned to the case. I had been an adoption specialist for four years when I met Travis. I worked in a small adoption agency specializing in special needs adoption. My caseload consisted of children that had gone through the foster care system, suffered abuse, and/or neglect, and whose parents had their parental rights terminated, freeing the children for adoption.

Local foster care agencies contract with this adoption agency to find adoptive homes for their children. When a foster care agency files a petition with the court to terminate parental rights, they ask our agency to recruit, study, and match families to children needing an adoptive home. Therefore, we recruit families, conduct home studies, and provide training for families interested in adoption.

We have many families already studied and approved waiting for the right child-match to happen. When a foster care agency makes a referral, we complete the child assessment and determine if one of our waiting families is a match for the child. If a match seems appropriate, we begin the adoption process. If there is not an appropriate family, we recruit a family for a particular child.

At our agency, we play another important role. Once a child comes under our supervision, we provide that child a therapist. Each of our adoptive specialists also provides therapy with adoptive children, adoptive families, and foster families, if necessary. Not every adopted child needs therapy. However, since all of our children suffered some form of abuse and/or neglect, most benefit from this service.

Questions

Before moving on in this case, examine the professional literature and local/state laws and policies about special needs adoptions in your state.

1. Does your state have a special needs adoption program? If so, what qualifies children as "special needs" adoption candidates?

2. From the professional literature, provide a description of a typical special needs adoptive child.

3. What is your state's adoption rate for these children? That is, are agencies in your state able to place special needs children in suitable adoptive homes? If not, where do these children end up in the system?

The Referral

When a foster care agency referred Travis to my agency, my supervisor assigned his case to me. Once assigned, I talked with the foster care worker to elicit as much information as possible about Travis's situation. Next, I read his foster care file. I wanted to know everything I could about the child to make the best match possible. Then I met with the foster parents because they lived with him and could paint the clearest picture of the child's needs. My final step was meeting the child to introduce myself, explain my role, what I will do for him, and the type of contact we will have. I followed this process with Travis.

Referral Information

Travis Evans was the only child born to Raymond and Shirley Evans. Travis was a healthy baby with no medical concerns. He was a bright, attentive baby that met all of his early developmental milestones. In the report, Ms. Evans stated that she gave birth to Travis while she was in the twelfth grade. She completed high school and immediately began working at Burger King. Soon thereafter, Shirley married Travis's father.

Ms. Evans also reported that Travis's primary caretakers during his early years were her alcoholic and depressed mother and her younger sister. Shirley visited with Travis on weekends and became his primary caretaker when he was approximately twelve to sixteen months old.

Ms. Evans said that her prenatal history was uneventful and she carried Travis full-term with no delivery complications. She reported his developmental milestones within normal limits. Travis's medical history showed no long-term illness. However, he did experience two hospitalizations. The first occurred when Travis was three or four years old. At that time, he took his maternal grandmother's heart medication and needed his stomach pumped. The second hospitalization occurred because of a blood infection. Ms. Evans described her infant/child as hyperactive, destructive with toys, and constantly active.

The Abuse Begins

As stated above, Travis's parents married shortly after his birth. Raymond (father) worked at a parts factory and Shirley worked in the home. Both Raymond and Shirley came from large families and they thought they wanted to have a large family too. However, early in Travis's life, trouble erupted in the Evans family. The parents began constantly fighting, yelling, and screaming at each other. Ms. Evans said there were incidents of domestic violence. In fact, she called the police to the house numerous times. The police arrested Raymond three times for battering Shirley. However, she dropped the charges each time.

Travis was not a bystander to the chaos in the family. As Travis grew up, the parents began redirecting their anger at each other toward Travis. First, they yelled at him for not answering as quickly as they thought he should. They began hitting him, punishing him for small mistakes, and telling him how dumb and stupid he was. Travis carried his problems at home to school, where he began acting out. Travis would fight other students, threaten smaller children, and steal from the teachers and bus drivers at school.

When Travis was 11 years old, during a fight Shirley threw the telephone at Raymond. However, it missed Raymond and hit Travis on the left side of his face, opening a large gash on the side of his face that they could not stop from bleeding. In addition to being hit by the telephone, when Travis's head hit the floor he was knocked unconscious. The parents called an ambulance to take Travis to the emergency room. When doctors and nurses examined him, they noticed numerous scars and bruises on his body. The medical staff believed that his parents had physically abused Travis over a long period. They immediately called CPS and made a child abuse report.

Later, the doctor testified that Raymond and Shirley physically abused Travis, and the abuse had occurred over a long period as demonstrated by the number of old scars on his body. The court referee removed Travis from his parents' custody and made him a temporary court ward, placing him in foster care. Mr. and Mrs. Evans needed to follow a court-ordered treatment plan if they wanted their son back. The parents continually denied any abuse and refused to work with the foster care worker, their attorney, or the court. After nine months, CPS filed a petition to terminate Raymond and Shirley's parental rights. The family court judge granted the petition, making Travis a permanent ward of the court and available for adoption.

Questions

Recently, many foster care systems across the United States have come under scrutiny for a variety of misdeeds, including misplaced children, abuse by foster parents, the lack of foster homes for children-of-color, and lengths of stay that are too long. However, any practitioner working with children and families will encounter the foster care system throughout their careers. Please respond to the following questions.

1. Examine your state's laws and policies regarding foster care and describe your state's foster care system.

2. From your investigation, how long are children usually in foster care in your state? How long can children remain in foster care before a permanency plan is put in place?

The Foster Home

CPS and his foster care worker placed Travis in the foster home of Daniel and Grace Miller. The Millers were an African American family with two biological sons, ages 13 and 15, living in the home. The Millers were both in their mid-40s and had been foster parents for ten years. Daniel and Grace were deeply religious people that wanted to give back to their community. They prayed about what they could do. They decided to become a foster home for children without families. Soon, the Millers received their foster care license after completing the approval process. In their ten years as foster parents, the Millers had 22 foster children in their home.

At the foster home, Travis appeared depressed. He continually asked when he could see his parents. He always wanted to know when he could go home. In the foster home, he demonstrated a number of behavioral problems including lying, stealing, and fighting. He experienced enuresis on a regular basis. Travis received medication, but it had little effect. He tried to start fights with the older boys in the home. Although the boys were bigger and stronger than Travis was, he did not seem to care. It appeared that Travis used the older boys to test his fighting skills before going to school.

Travis also acted out in the school; before, during, and after school Travis had problems. He fought, engaged in inappropriate behavior, and disrespected his teachers. In the classroom, Travis was disruptive when he did not get his way.

Questions

Travis presented with significant behavioral problems after living with abusive parents. Based on the information you have at this point, answer the following questions before moving ahead with this case.

1. **What is your first hunch regarding the presenting problem? Explore the practice literature and discuss this issue with other students to find the prevalence of this type of behavior among abused children in foster care. If the literature does not speak specifically about this problem, are there other problems or categories of problems that this behavior fits with pertaining to treatment?**

2. **What is the next direction of inquiry and assessment? Based on the practice literature, what information would you need to collect to perform a comprehensive and/or multi-systemic assessment? (See Chapter 1.)**

3. **What personal strengths can you locate and name at this early juncture in treatment? Make a preliminary list of Travis's problems and strengths.**

Meeting Travis

The foster care worker and I met with Travis at the foster home. Our agency policy mandated that we meet clients where they were most comfortable. By the time we met, Travis had been living with the Millers for almost a year, so we thought that would be the most appropriate place to meet. The foster care worker introduced me and stayed for the first meeting. By having the foster care worker with me, it gave Travis permission to talk to someone else. Travis had difficulty forming relationships and difficulty relating to other adults. Travis might not have accepted me had the foster care worker skipped our first meeting.

Travis presented as a small boy, who appeared below average in height and weight. He looked about 5 feet tall and weighted no more than 100 pounds. He looked nervous and maintained most of his eye contact with the foster care worker.

The foster care worker introduced me and explained why I was there. I talked with Travis about our adoption agency, my role, and how we could work together. I also talked about adoptive families and how they treat children. We spent the remainder of the first meeting talking about games, toys, and sports that he liked.

The next several meetings focused on adoption, what he wanted in adoptive parents, and how I could help find a family for him. By giving children a role in the adoption, they are more likely to invest in the process. I asked Travis what he liked about his foster family. He first mentioned his room, toys, and people to play with. As we continued to meet, he talked about foods he liked, going to the movies, and playing family games. Finally, he talked about what he liked about the foster parents. When trying to match a family to Travis, it would be helpful if the family could do a couple of things on Travis's list to assist with the transition to a new home.

Questions

Preparing children for adoption can be a difficult task. They may still have ties to their biological parents, and children sometimes believe that acceptance of the adoptive parents means they betrayed or rejected their biological parents.

1. What are some ways that you could help a child understand that adoption is not a rejection of his or her biological parents?

2. The child may want to know why his parents did not fight to get him back. The child may internalize the rejection as something he did to make his parents leave. How would you work with the child for him to understand that his parents did not reject him?

The Adoptive Parent

The adoptive mother I located was Ms. Debra Wright. Ms. Wright was an African American 31-year-old. She worked as a secretary in a business office. Ms. Wright married once at the age of 20. She met her husband in college and quit school when they married. She wanted her husband to finish college so he could provide for the family. Two years after college and three years after they first married, her husband filed for divorce.

With the separation and then divorce looming, Ms. Wright found a job as a secretary. After awhile, she began to enjoy her job and made friends. She received a couple of promotions. Debra stated that she had hoped to find the right person, try marriage a second time, and start a family. As she reached age 30, she was no longer sure about the new relationship, but knew she wanted a family. Her employer supported and promoted adoption as one of his charitable causes. He provided Debra information on adoption, and provided financial resources to anyone who wanted to adopt. After talking with her family about it, Ms. Wright decided to become an adoptive parent. She had two sisters, three brothers, and a mother and father who were not only supportive of her adopting, but all stated they would help her and the child. With that information in hand, Ms. Wright contacted my adoption agency.

Questions

1. Each state has it own ways of handling adoption. In your state, what are the steps for adopting an infant, international child, and an older child? When answering, look at things such as fees, court costs, attorney fees, legal requirements; age, gender, marital status; and income as factors that could decide if someone could adopt.

2. Locate businesses in your community that provide adoption benefits. Discuss what types of benefits are available and if they provide the support that people who want to adopt require.

Assessment

Ms. Wright experienced the same problems with Travis, as did his foster parents. I served as his therapist during the adoption process, and continued in that role while he adjusted to the Wright home. Ms. Wright reported that Travis was manipulative, difficult to discipline, and easily frustrated when he did not get the attention he sought at home or school. She also reported that Travis's behavior problems included aggressive threats toward peers and adults, acting out, stealing, lying and enuresis, the last incident being approximately a month earlier in the classroom. His mother felt that Travis deliberately urinated on himself in school because he wanted to return to his self-contained classroom, although he was capable of completing all academic tasks in the general education program. A school psychologist diagnosed Travis with Attention Deficit Disorder (ADD) and their doctor prescribed Ritalin.

Ms. Wright also said that Travis's problems had existed for several years, but had intensified in the adoptive home. She stated that Travis had difficulties at school and in social relationships, which resulted in low self-esteem and delayed emotional development. Travis took no ownership for his behavior and acted out inappropriately with others as a mechanism to get attention. Furthermore, Ms. Wright wondered what he knew about his father and how that was influencing his behavior. Travis's father was serving a life sentence in state prison for double murder. The case was heavily reported in the media and kids at school teased and harassed him about this incident.

During our meetings, Travis identified that he had problems with peer relationships and only had two close friends at school. In the community, he had one neighbor friend with whom he went out at night looking for dogs or cats to shoot with his friend's new B.B. gun. Travis said that he liked watching television and videos that illustrated violent and aggressive acts. He indicated that he recalled watching movies with themes of violence since his early school years.

Regarding his depressive symptomology, Travis said that he "thinks he likes himself," but has often thought about hurting himself. He said that he loved to draw and wanted to make his mom proud of him. Travis said he felt lonely and spent most of his time in his bedroom, though on occasions he may invite his neighbor over to play with his Play Station. He indicated that he "gets bored" with his friend and has asked him to leave on at least two occasions. He did not participate in extracurricular activities at school. Travis spent most of his time going to the grocery store with his mother and visiting his grandparents.

Travis described his family as "nice," but wished his mother let him make some of his own choices. He also said that he did not want to attend all the family activities because he liked to stay home. He expressed themes of anger, abandonment, and low self-esteem.

Questions

Now that the author has presented Travis's personal history and before reading further, perform the following exercises based on your education, experience, the professional literature, and best practice evidence. To increase the learning potential of this exercise, you may want to do this in a small group with other students.

1. Based on the information contained above, construct a three-generation genogram and eco-map that represent Travis's personal, familial, and environmental circumstances. What further information do you need to complete this exercise? What patterns do these two important graphical assessment tools demonstrate?

2. Develop a list of Travis's problems and strengths. Include his family in this list.

3. Write a three-page narrative assessment that encompasses Travis's multisystemic issues and strengths. Review Chapter 1, if needed. This narrative should provide a comprehensive and multi-systemic explanation of his life as he undergoes therapy with the author.

4. Try to identify the theoretical model or approach that you used to guide your assessment. According to the literature, what other theoretical options are available and how would these change the nature of your assessment?

5. End by developing multi-axial DSM-IV-TR diagnoses for Travis. Be sure to look for evidence of multiple diagnoses on Axis I. Provide the list of client symptoms that you used to justify your diagnostic decisions. What, if any, information was missing that would make this an easier task?

6. Based on your determination, plan your approach for treatment. What initial goals would you have in treatment? What steps would you take to ensure that your treatment addressed the needs of Travis, his family, and the adoption agency?

Course of Treatment

As I continued meeting with Travis, I used various forms of interventions including therapeutic games, drawings, and individual and group sessions. Travis began feeling comfortable with sharing his feelings. Travis expressed that he did not like his peers in his school and had only two friends. He said that he did not get along with others because they talked about his clothes and hair, and made fun of him because he had body odor. He said that his teacher sent him to the office a lot and he was suspended because of his fighting and disrespect for authority figures.

Travis also questioned my gender. He said that he did not think I could help him because he needed a male therapist to explain his development as a boy. It was apparent that Travis struggled with issues regarding his masculinity and his need to form attachments with others. He wanted to know where he fit in the world. Simultaneously, he wanted to cling to and be close to his mother. However, at the same time, he wanted to make independent choices. Travis's strengths: (1) he had not involved himself in delinquent behaviors, which suggested that he had not lost his identity; (2) he had not lost his own personality and did not want to lose it; and (3) he was able to struggle for his individuality.

Therapeutic Model

Object relations theory has an extensive range of applications and explores the relationship between being separate and independent from others and the need to form attachments with others. It describes the development of an infant's earliest relationships, primarily in the mother-child dyad. It utilizes elements of different theories that explore relationships with real external people and internal mental representations as well as internal images of self (Greenberg & Mitchell, 1983, Flanagan, 1996). The concept of object relations originated in Freud's (1938, 1939) drive model, which suggests that an object can be real or imagined and hold significance for the individual (Strean, 1996). Margaret Mahler, whose theory of separation-individuation originates in the drive model but focuses on the environmental system, developed her work into a new psychological developmental process. Mahler emphasized the concept of object relations. For example,

> Her account of the child's immersion in symbolic fusion with his mother and of a gradual, halting emergence from that fusion into independent self-hood has provided a generation of analytic theorists and practitioners with a version of the essential struggles of childhood which is quite different from Freud's. (Greenberg & Mitchell, 1983, p. 272)

Mahler describes her theory of separation-individuation as a series of chronological phases, each necessary and affecting how a child moves through the developmental sequences while being influenced by external factors (Edward, Ruskin, & Turrini, 1981). The terms *separation-individuation* are key components in her theory. Separation refers to differentiation, distancing, and the process of emancipating from mother. Individuation refers to autonomy and independence, the development of a unique self.

Moreover, Mahler proposed the following developmental phases that adolescents must encounter and master if they are to become well-adjusted adolescents.

Autistic Phase

The phase of normal autism takes place during the time of birth and the first month, which precedes the evolution to symbiosis (Mahler, Pine, & Bergman, 1975). The infant is unable to distinguish self from mother, but is able to separate pleasurable from painful experiences with the primary goal being satisfaction and homeostasis. Mahler refers to this stage as primary narcissism when there is no awareness of another or of an outside. "It is as if the infant experiences himself or herself as the source of his/her own satisfaction, self-sufficient and omnipotent" (Edward et al., 1981, p. 4). Other developmental theorists such as Stern (1985) have criticized this phase of development, believing that, at birth, the infant has the capacity to relate to others.

Another critical point in this phase is the concept described by Bowles (1988), which points out that for ethnically diverse parents specifically, "black mother's feelings about herself and her infant, with which her feelings of blackness are inextricably tied, are experienced by the infant" (Bowles, 1988, p. 107). In other words, if black parents can identify who they are in terms of identity and how they view themselves in the world, they can instill in their infant/child what it means to be black with a sense of pride (Bowles, 1988).

Symbiotic Phase

According to Mahler, Pine, and Bergman (1975), the symbiotic phase is a prerequisite to all other subsequent human relations. It describes that state of undifferentiation, of fusion with mother, in which the "I" is not yet differentiated from the "not-I," and in which inside and outside are gradually coming to be sensed as different (Mahler et al., 1975, p. 44). The mother serves as an auxiliary ego or a protective shield as defined by Spitz (1965), because the infant is unable to manage frustration or tension and needs the mother to serve as an object.

During this period, the concept of the holding environment is of much significance because the mother protects the infant and reassures him/her a safe place in the world. This is also a time when the infant begins to exhibit unspecific smiling responses, which can continue throughout the differentiation phase. The distinction of these smiling responses are viewed differently when the infant at two months smiles at the sight of a human face, compared to the mother's face between the ages of 4–5 months. These particular smiling responses are forms of connectiveness—the capacity to develop interactions with others which is the hallmark of socialization (Edward et al., 1981).

Separation-Individuation Proper

Mahler states that the infant begins to "hatch" out of symbiosis and enters the phase separation-individuation proper which consists of the following subphases: (1) differentiation, (2) practicing, (3) rapprochement, and (4) object constancy.

Differentiation (5–10 months). During this phase, the infant/child begins to compare mother with others as he/she begins to separate self from mother. A growing interest in the outside world is present as the child begins to crawl, roll and stand, exploring and taking risks. The child is more observant of the mother's face and body through touch, sight, and smell. The phenomena of "stranger anxiety" also develops in this phase as the child is often seen scanning the room for the mother. This illustrates that the child is beginning to know the face of the mother from others—has begun to individuate and sees mother as a separate self object. Mahler further asserts that "this phenomenon and the factors underlying its variations constitute an important aspect of and clue to our evaluation of the libidinal object, of socialization, and the first step towards emotional object constancy" (Mahler, Pine, & Bergman, 1975, p. 226).

Practicing (10–15 months). Mahler, Pine, and Bergman (1975) emphasize this phase as a time that the child begins to differentiate himself/herself with the intensified maturation of locomotive skills. This is a time of grandiosity, omnipotence, and narcissism. Although the child is beginning to explore the world and the environment more—which is the beginning of autonomy—the mother continues to serve as a home base or refueling object in order to fulfill the child's physical needs.

Transitional objects, according to Mahler, describe an inanimate object used by the child as a representation or symbolization of the mother. The object can be a blanket, teddy bear, pacifier, or even a bedtime song that serves as a symbol of the mother. Essentially the "transitional object represents a way station and will finally be decathected, which is to say, it will lose its importance when the child can begin to perform soothing operations for itself without the need for an illusory external soother" (Edward et al., 1981, p. 22).

Edward, Ruskin, and Turrini (1981) further report that the father in this phase can be viewed as the other, and not just a secondary mother surrogate, as the child continues to differentiate himself/herself. This phase of practice has two parts, consisting of an early and late practicing phase. Bowles (1988) further asserts that black parents in this phase should incorporate the concept of color (race) as the child begins to experience his/her whole body. "Although the concept of color is not present for the child at this age, its inclusion lays the groundwork for positive ethnic affirmation" (Bowles, 1988, p. 108).

Rapprochement (15–22 months). This is a time when the child has opposing needs—a back and forth movement of dependence and autonomy. The child needs to be close but seeks separateness as he/she explores the world alone. However, this is a period of time that the child seeks the emotional availability of the mother. As the child's cognitive abilities and ego apparatus continue to develop, the child has an increased desire for the mother to share in his/her world, by involving her with every activity of play that he/she experiences. An increase in language development, symbolic play, and communication continue to be present as the child distinguishes from "good self" and "bad self" as well as good and bad object(s) (Mahler et al., 1975). For black children, Bowles (1988) recommends that afro-centric toys be incorporated into the child's play because it helps the child identify who he/she is in terms of color and in other social and cultural situations.

Object Constancy. Mahler and colleagues (1975) explain that this last subphase has two distinctions, which are (1) "the achievement of a definite, and in certain aspects, lifelong, individuality, and (2) the attainment of a certain degree of object constancy" (p. 109). This phase also incorporates the child's ability to internalize good and bad objects into self-representations as well as the mother.

Questions

The author proposes using object-relations theory to treat Travis. This theory is well known and is taught in most schools of social work across the United States. However, as a practice theory, object-relations is less popular than in previous years, primarily because it does not fit well under managed care limitations. That is, object-relations therapy is normally considered a long-term, insight-oriented therapy derived from Freud's work in psychoanalysis. Hence, most managed care operations, whether concerning private or public funding for treatment, would not approve treatment lengths that fit this theory. Please respond to the following questions before reading further.

1. Examine the practice literature about object-relations theory and describe this theory and how practitioners use it in therapy. Discuss how object-relations theory specifically relates to Travis's situation and use that theory to assess Travis's current condition.

2. Why do you think that the adoption worker's focus on Travis's history to address his current situation is more effective than trying to change his behaviors?

3. Given what you know about this case and based on the professional practice literature, what other theories or models of treatment could help Travis and his situation? Please explain.

4. Based on your research and experience, what theory or model would you use with Travis if you were his therapist?

Object-Relations Theory and Travis

According to Mahler's developmental schema, Travis presented as a latency-age boy who was developmentally fixated in several phases of development. The mixed messages that his biological mother sent by not allowing him to grow and now the absence of both parents, forced him to regress to earlier stages of development. He identified with the maternal object instead of the father as his new object. According to Lucente (1996), in the overall context of individuation, the task for the male identifying with mother depends on the psychological similarity of the father. The lack of a good enough mother, a concept first used by Winnicott (1953), suggests that because of his biological parents' psychological struggles and Travis's caretaking needs being supplied by his maternal depressed, alcoholic grandmother, some of Travis's basic needs for growth, tolerance, and frustration affected his psychic structure.

Travis seemed partly in the symbiotic phase of development because he continued to see his mother as auxiliary ego or a protective shield without being aware of separateness. His placement back into his self-contained classroom symbolized a holding environment where he felt safe in the school system. Travis's difficulty with social and personal relationships suggested that he wanted to "get even" or "get ahead" in social situations. In other words, as stated by Masterson (1972), Travis feared abandonment and engulfment.

Travis also seemed in the first steps of the rapprochement phase as he had opposing needs to be close to and yet separate from his mother. In the treatment relationship with me, Travis was in the practicing phase. I had become a significant, maternal, and growth-producing object that helped him grow and evaluate himself. The quality of the relationship and the significance of his meaning-making narratives represented the social constructivist perspective, which takes into account his social and cultural experiences.

To understand Travis's reality, I needed to understand how he shared his representational worldview in treatment. By allowing Travis to discuss past and current experiences in relation to his life, he could examine how these events constructed his identity and shaped his meaning-making activity (Sarri, 1991) and his ability to create new meaning systems in his life.

Question

In the previous exercises, in Question 1 you were asked to apply object-relations theory to Travis's current situation. How did your application of the theory compare to the author's? What is your professional opinion of this theory's applicability to Travis and his need for professional help?

Social Constructionism

Social constructionism is a postmodern paradigm that examines multiple belief systems and perspectives (Gonzalez, Biever, & Gardner, 1994) (see Chapter 1). Gergen (1994) explains that social constructionism evaluates human interactions and the sources of interactive exchanges. Individuals with a postmodern framework believe that there are many possible realities in evaluating human behavior and social exchanges. Overall, postmodern thinkers agree that knowledge is subjective and is only determined through multiple circumstances (Rubin, 1997). Social constructionism postulates that meanings are fluid, flexible, and always changing (Gonzalez, Biever, & Gardner, 1994).

According to Shawver (1996), this postmodern thought has two parts: "a deconstructive part that shows us that old ways of seeing things are limited or wrong, and a constructive part that enables our imaginations to construct new and useful ways of thinking" (p. 372). In essence, this new way of thinking allows social workers to evaluate old ways of arriving at truths and suggests new structures that include the process of language.

Shawver (1996) points out that postmodernism offers psychoanalysis a new set of propositions to study and observe as part of the psychoanalytic process. Gonzalez, Biever, and Gardner (1994) suggest that social constructionism is compatible with a multicultural perspective in counseling diverse populations. Social constructionism relates to this multicultural perspective because it also evaluates social and cultural issues in the experience of one's environmental system.

Working from a social constructionist perspective, practitioners explore clients' understanding of their behaviors and experiences as they construct their own meaning-making narratives, rather than focusing on how clients fit into the therapist's theoretical orientation. The application of a social constructionist approach in treatment suggests that diagnostic labeling is one evaluation inventory with many possible ways of understanding human behavior. In other words, practitioners working with ethnic diverse populations, but specifically with African American male adolescents, should note that some behavior patterns might appear as diagnostic criteria for DSM-IV-TR categorizing. However, these behaviors may actually be nonpathological and means of survival for adolescents living in the inner city.

Social constructionist thinkers recommend that instead of expanding existing diagnostic categories, practitioners should explore clients' meaning and behavior from a social and cultural position (Gonzalez, Biever, & Gardner, 1994). Other clinical applications in this paradigm reveal that practitioners should consider themselves as learners. This emphasis implies that experts cannot inform clients about how they view their world. In addition, clients' ability to construct and reconstruct their stories in a social constructionist's lens is considered a hypothesis instead of their dominant understanding of themselves (Gonzalez, Biever, & Gardner, 1994).

Using this paradigm in a postmodern approach has many merits, but there are also some challenges. According to Gonzalez, Biever, and Gardner (1994), these challenges include (1) ideas of client(s) that have no empirical base, but make sense for them, (2) fluid and changing truths that pose a problem in understanding science, and (3) abandoning the therapist as an expert. However, Gergen (1994) states that "social constructionism invites new forms of inquiry, substantially expanding the scope and significance of the endeavors of human science" (p. 30).

Questions

The author expanded her theoretical base to include social constructionism, primarily as a way to include multicultural considerations in therapy. She also included notions about the importance of empirical science when presenting potential problems with social constructionism.

1. The author discussed how social constructionism could be applied with Travis. Discuss her rationale and explain the strengths and weaknesses of her argument.

2. Explore the evidence-based practice literature about the importance of empirically based models and methods versus ideas gained from practice wisdom. What is the emerging position of the social work profession regarding these two sources of knowledge? Based on your findings, what is your position on the issue? Explain your ideas in the context of the literature and professional practice.

Clinical Implications

Although Mahler's paradigm seems useful for assessing early developmental failure and can be used with clients struggling with many issues, it seems a better fit for Caucasian adolescents who struggle to belong in families and become autonomous individuals. However, the African American adolescents have two additional burdens: (1) how to get out of family dependency but continue to have close ties, and (2) how to survive in a society where oppressive and racist ideologies exist. Social constructionism seems more useful because it incorporates language meaning and the environment system in the treatment relationship. Mahler and social constructionism only seem compatible if Mahler's theory of development further examines infants from diverse backgrounds, evaluates interpersonal interactions, and provides a more internalized process for evaluating human behavior.

Evaluation of Theoretical Paradigms and African American Adolescents

I presented the theoretical paradigms to evaluate Mahler's developmental schema and social constructionism with the focus on social work as a theory of science. The question remains: are these paradigms compatible in the treatment process? Before discussing these constructs completely, it is important to understand the unique issues involved with treating African American children/adolescent males.

The process of seeking mental health services emerges as complex phenomena for all minority and culturally diverse populations, but especially for African American males living in inner-cities (Cannio & Sprulock, 1994). In addition, for some African American families, mental health services bring many stereotypes. Clinicians working in the inner-city who treat African American and other diverse populations must be aware of the sociocultural aspects between practitioners and clients that affect the treatment relationship. This statement recognizes that the development of professional relationships is a two-person exchange—a joining process that evaluates language, meaning, and attunement based on human experience with roots in social constructionist philosophy. Gabarino (1993) notes that it is important to understand that an inner-city child's coping abilities are mechanisms for survival and help determine a child's meaning system.

Adolescence itself is a stressor, especially for children living in environments with violence and drugs (Blos, 1983). Adolescents are often filled with raging self-doubt, altering with unrealistic omnipotence; the adolescent's ability to differentiate between thought, wish, impulse, and action is compromised. I drew this from work by Erickson (1963) to suggest that the task of trust versus mistrust at infancy and the establishment of one's own identity through adulthood is part of normal development.

Regardless of how an African American adolescent goes through the process of development, he/she cannot escape racial prejudices. For African American male adolescents, many challenges await him regarding his role in society; however, his family and extended support system can serve as a resource during his time of development.

According to Majors and Billson (1992), the term "cool pose" illustrates how black males see their roles, self-representations, interactions with others, meaning system and physical body structure, along with how they are interchangeable in representing black masculinity. The process of understanding black masculinity and adolescent development is vital in the treatment relationship. In terms of clinical application, Jones (1985) presents four useful variables: (1) reactions to racial oppression, (2) majority culture expectations, (3) African American culture, and (4) experiences that involve self and family members.

Questions

The author provided an in-depth discussion about the role of object-relations theory in the work with adolescent males. The adoption worker makes a distinction in the model for working with Caucasian and African American adolescent males.

1. From the author's discussion of object-relations theory, discuss Mahler's developmental schema, which includes the autistic phase, symbiotic phase, and the separation-individual proper and its importance in understanding adolescent development.

2. Make an argument about why this model may not be the most effective treatment model for African American males.

Case Summary

In the preceding pages, I described Travis and his current situation in significant detail. This account of my work takes you through the first seven months of what became a two-year professional relationship. At this stage of treatment, treatment really began. It took that long to develop the kind of relationship I needed to work toward change. Unfortunately, Travis's case is common, as was the process we went through to develop a relationship. That is, by focusing on rapport and engagement during the early stages of therapy instead of confrontation, intervention planning, and change, even young troubled African American boys can progress from what some would call resistant to what I call engaged, willing partners in the therapeutic process.

However, at this stage of the case, our work is not complete—not even close. This is where you come in. It is now your task to work with Travis and his demons. As you move forward planning for the remainder of the case, do not be fooled into believing that the level of engagement and commitment Travis exhibited to this point is permanent. My experience says that it is one thing to engage clients to the point where they will relive and relate their lives. This is the "easy" part. It is a different task entirely to help clients deepen their commitment to themselves and take concrete steps toward a new life. Under your care, Travis is about to confront his own dilemma of change (Johnson, 2004). That is, Travis has choices, none of which will appear promising from his perspective at this moment in his life. It is your job as practitioners to help him find his way from this point forward, keeping in mind that the relationship will have to build with every step of the process, or treatment will likely fail.

This is the point in Travis's case where you take over. What happens next? I am passing Travis to you for completion. Good Luck!

Assessment, Diagnoses, and Treatment Planning

Here, your job is to develop and write a comprehensive narrative assessment of Travis's life, family, and environment. Your narrative assessment should reflect the multi-systemic information gleaned during the case and build on the assessment you began earlier. It should also include information I provided above in the discussion of Travis's situation from an object-relations perspective. The multi-systemic narrative assessment becomes the client's case history report (Johnson, 2004) and includes a comprehensive diagnostic statement that integrates essential client information into a coherent description of her life, history, and current circumstances. The case history report concludes with a multi-axial DSM (APA, 2000) diagnosis (or, in this case perhaps, multiple diagnoses), and/or a Person-In-Environment (PIE) score (Karls & Wandrei, 1994a, 1994b). There is a debate within social work about the pros and cons of the DSM diagnostic system that is outside the scope of this text. To review these issues, I encouraged you to look elsewhere (Johnson, 2004; Glicken, 2004; Kirk & Kutchins, 1992).

The multi-systemic case history report should lead directly to a multi-systemic and multi-modal written treatment plan (Johnson, 2004) that is understandable and agreeable to your client. This plan should include your client as a full partner in the process. This will be especially important in Travis's case, given the importance of African American males being partners in the treatment process (Franklin, 1992). There are many formats available to develop treatment plans (Johnson, 2004; Perkinson & Jongsma, 1998); use whatever format you want to enhance your learning in this case.

Questions

1. Finish drawing the three-generation genogram that you began earlier. Also, develop an eco-map that best represents Travis's involvement with multiple social systems and organizations in his environment.

2. Make a list, with supporting evidence, of the main issues in Travis's life at this moment. Include several of his personal and environmental strengths that pertain to each of the issues you listed.

3. Develop a written multi-systemic case history report complete with diagnostic statement. Determine Travis's multi-axial (Five axes and GAF scores) DSM diagnosis, or multiple diagnoses if indicated. Be sure that the information contained in the case history report clearly defends your diagnostic decisions. It is not appropriate to base diagnostic decisions on assumptions, only on direct

evidence provided by your client. In addition, you may apply the PIE classification system to determine his level of social functioning.

- **If you were to meet with Travis, what additional information would you need to contribute to a more holistic comprehensive case history report?**
- **Be sure to make whatever strengths Travis may have a central part of the case history report and diagnoses.**

4. Based on the case history report, develop a written treatment plan that includes short- and long-term treatment goals. Include what methods of treatment and support you will utilize.

- **What treatment theory or combination of theories do you believe best fits Travis and his reality? Defend your decision.**
- **What theories or approaches does the latest empirical evidence in the field recommend?**

Intervention Planning and Implementation

Based on the comprehensive case history report and written treatment plan developed above, it is now time to decide on intervention strategies.

Based on the treatment theory or theories chosen and defended above, list each intervention you would use in your work with Travis. Specifically, for each intervention, include the target issue, intervention and modality (i.e., group therapy) you chose, and the theoretical justification for each.

1. What other options might be available should these interventions prove ineffective?
2. What does the latest empirical evidence in the field suggest for each target issue? How does this evidence match with your intervention strategies?
3. When developing treatment approaches do not overlook nontraditional approaches and approaches that target multiple systemic levels (i.e., individual, family, community, advocacy, etc.).
4. What factors and strategies will you use to build trust and engagement during the intervention phases of your work? How will you assist Travis as his motivation for change waxes and wanes over the coming weeks and months?

Termination, Aftercare, and Follow-Up

Preparing for termination begins early in the treatment process. Proper termination includes many factors, beside how your client progresses in treatment. Hence, this exercise will help you think about the various issues that go into successful termination, aftercare, and follow-up.

Questions

1. List and explain the general factors to consider in developing a successful aftercare plan for adopted clients.

2. List and explain the issues in Travis's life to consider when planning for termination and aftercare.

3. What indicators (Travis's progress in treatment) will you use to determine when it is an appropriate time for termination?

4. Plan a specific strategy for termination, aftercare, and follow-up that best fits Travis's reality and professional standards of practice. What does the latest empirical evidence in the field say about these issues?

Evaluation of Practice

Evaluation is important to the practice process. Preparing to evaluate Travis's progress in treatment must begin during the early stages of therapy. Evaluative efforts not only allow practitioners to know how their clients are progressing, areas where you need to change your approach, and when it might be appropriate to terminate treatment, but also contribute to the knowledge base of the field and profession. Additionally, most funding sources—private and public—require evidence of practice evaluation and documentation of client outcome. Therefore, developing methods for practice evaluation are essential. Now, this is your task.

Questions

1. Based on your knowledge of research and evaluation methods, develop a plan for practice evaluation that measures both practice process and client outcome.

2. Explain the rationale for your approach and how both targets (process and outcome) are integrated to give an overall evaluation of your practice efforts with Travis.

Bibliography

American Psychiatric Association (2000). *Diagnostic and statistical manual of mental disorders* (4th ed., TR). Washington, DC: Author.

Blos, R. (1983). The contribution of psychoanalysis to the psychotherapy of adolescents. In A. J. Solnit, R. S. Eissler, & P. B. Neubauer (eds.), *The psychoanalytic study of the child, 38*. New Haven, CT: Yale University Press.

Bowles, D. (1988). Development of an ethnic self-concept among blacks. In C. Jacobs, & D. Bowles (eds.), *Ethnicity and race: Critical concepts in social work*. Washington, DC: NASW Press.

Cannio, I., & Sprulock, J. (1994). *Culturally diverse children and adolescents.* New York: Guilford Press.

Edward, J., Ruskin, N., & Turrini, P. (1981). *Separation-individuation: Theory and application.* New York: Gardner Press.

Erickson, E. H. (1963). *Childhood and society* (3rd ed.). New York: Norton.

Flanagan, L. M. (1996). Object relations theory. In J. Berzoff, L. Flanagan, & P. Hertz (eds.). *Inside and outside in.* New York: Jason Aronson.

Franklin, A. J. (1992). Therapy with African American men. *Families in Society: The Journal of Contemporary Human Services,* 350–355.

Freud, S. (1939). *An outline of psychoanalysis.* London: Hegarth Press.

Freud, S. (1938). *The basic writings of Sigmund Freud.* New York: Random House.

Gabarino, J. (1993). Children's response to community violence: What do we know? *Infant Mental Health Journal, 14*(2), 103–115.

Gergen, K. (1994). *Realities and relationships: Soundings in social constructionism.* Cambridge, MA: Harvard University Press.

Glicken, M. D. (2004). *Using the strengths perspective in social work practice.* Boston: Allyn and Bacon.

Gonzalez, R., Biever, J., & Gardner, G. (1994). The multicultural perspective in therapy: A social constructionist approach. *Psychotherapy, 31*(3), 515–524.

Greenberg, J. R., & Mitchell, S. (1983). *Object relations in psychoanalytic theory.* Cambridge, MA: Harvard University Press.

Johnson, J. L. (2004). *Fundamentals of substance abuse practice.* Belmont, CA: Thomson-Brooks/Cole.

Karls, J., & Wandrei, K. (1994a). *Person-in-environment system: The PIE classification system for functioning problems.* Washington, DC: NASW.

Karls, J., & Wandrei, K. (1994b). *PIE manual: Person-in-environment system: The PIE classification system for social functioning.* Washington, DC: NASW.

Kirk, S. A., & Kutchins, H. (1992). *The selling of DSM: The rhetoric of science in psychiatry.* Beverly Hills, CA: Sage.

Lucente, R. (1996). Sexual identity: Conflict and confusion in a male adolescent. *Child and Adolescent Social Work, 13*(2), 97–114.

Mahler, S., Pine, F., & Bergman, A. (1975). *The psychological birth of the human infant.* New York: Basic Books.

Majors, R., & Billson, J. (1992). *Cool pose: The dilemmas of black manhood in America.* New York: Lexington.

Masterson, J. (1972). *Treatment of the borderline adolescent: A developmental approach.* New York: Wiley.

Perkinson, R. R., & Jongsma, A. E., Jr. (1998). *The chemical dependence treatment planner.* New York: Wiley.

Rubin, S. (1997). Self and object in the postmodern world. *Psychotherapy, 34*(1), 1–10.

Sarri, C. (1991). *The creation of meaning in clinical social work.* New York: Guilford Press.

Shawver, L. (1996). What postmodernism can do for psychoanalysis. *The American Journal of Psychoanalysis, 56*(4), 371–393.

Spitz, R. A. (1965). *The first year of life: A psychoanalytic study of normal and deviant development of object relations.* New York: International Universities Press.

Stern, D. (1985). *The interpersonal world of the infant.* New York: Basic Books.

Strean, H. (1996). Psychoanalytic theory and social work treatment. In F. Turner (ed.), *Social work treatment* (4th ed.). New York: The Free Press.

Winnicott, D. (1953). Transitional objects and transitional phenomena: A study of the first not-me possession. *The International Journal of Psychoanalysis, 34,* 89–97.